The Maritime Photographs of
Francis Frith

W.J. West

Published by

Waterfront Publications

A division of Nicholas Smith International Limited

7 Salisbury Street, Blandford Forum, Dorset DT11 7AU

Telephone: 0258 459535   Fax: 0258 459655   Telex: 417154 NSMITH G

Contents

© Text W.J. West, Photographs National Maritime Museum
ISBN 0 946184 73 9   1993
Typeset by PageMerger, Southampton, Hampshire
Printed by The Amadeus Press, Huddersfield, West Yorkshire

FRANCIS FRITH – HISTORICAL BACKGROUND

This book contains a selection of some 130 superb photographs from a collection which was slowly accumulated through the Victorian era and in the end numbered hundreds of thousands. The vast majority of the photographs were preserved in the form of original, large, glass-plate negatives, still in remarkably good condition considering that the photographs were often taken and processed in the field on the tours Frith made to every part of the country. Inevitably, over the years, many were destroyed when Frith made fresh tours over the same routes taking new views as the appearance of the country rapidly changed to replace the old. The collection which now survives numbers over sixty thousand and this is split into two main collections: the maritime photographs and the remainder. There are over a thousand maritime photographs and these are housed in the National Maritime Museum at Greenwich, near London, an entirely appropriate place for them to be.

Although the photographs here are taken exclusively from the Greenwich collection, the fullest cooperation has been extended by those now holding the Francis Frith collection in Shaftesbury where the bulk of Frith's surviving prints are housed. Anyone wishing to understand the breadth of Frith's achievement needs only to look at that archive where, through the excellent facilities available, the public may still obtain prints from the original negatives produced with just the same skill and prompt service that Frith offered more than a hundred years ago. The collections together cover every single inhabited place in the United Kingdom and nearly all the notable views and monuments as well.

It may well be asked what sort of person conceived such an extraordinary project and had the will and tenacity to see it through. To answer this question with a short biographical sketch such as that which follows is perhaps inadequate, but it will be supplemented with other remarks where relevant in the text, and in the captions to the images.

Francis Frith was born in Chesterfield in 1822. He was of Quaker stock, his father being a cooper, and he remained a Quaker all his life. He went to school in Birmingham but was unhappy there and equally unhappy in a trade apprenticeship he took up, finally having to break it for a period suffering from what has later been described as a nervous breakdown. When this happened his parents took him on a tour of England which seems to have been a seminal event in his life. After finishing his apprenticeship he went into business, first in partnership and then on his own in Liverpool which had begun its great period of expansion through the trans-atlantic trade established by Cunard and others. It is not known exactly what these earlier businesses were, but while still very young he started another business, this time in printing, at which he was particularly successful. He sold this business when only thirty-four and became a gentleman of leisure. We do not know how much he realized from this sale, but his business was turning over £200,000 a year, an immense sum at that time, at least £10 million in modern terms, probably more.

With his freedom, and ample resources gained by his own efforts, Frith decided to follow the impulse to travel which had been formed all those years before when his parents took him round the country. This time however he went abroad and travelled on a grand scale, acting both as explorer and photographer, going in search, it seems, of the origin of the Nile and to look at the holy places in Palestine.

His interest in photography had developed as the science of photography had developed. His photographs, laboriously produced from large glass-plate negatives using the wet-plate process with equipment which had to be taken everywhere by camel, created a sensation when they arrived back in London. They were widely exhibited and published on a grand scale in a large folio issued in twenty-five parts at ten shillings each, with the title *Egypt and Palestine Photographed and Described*. The book was illustrated with actual photographs laid down on to the page, as was the custom in those days, and achieved mass circulation. No modern-day book could hope to compete with it. When Frith returned to England he decided to settle down and, although he toured the Continent frequently, never went on formal explorations again. He

The frozen Thames at Gravesend in February 1895. All have been caught in the ice's grip, from the fishing boats inshore to every kind of steam and sailing vessel. The ships in the background look for all the world as if they are in a Dutch old master painting.

married and went to live in Reigate where he set up the photographic business that was to become the largest of its kind in the world. Exactly when he conceived his great idea of visiting and photographing every spot in the country is not known. The idea of *describing* every place in the country was not new. It had been attempted in the great Elizabethan topographical works such as Camden's *Britannia* illustrated with Speed's famous maps. The latest in this kind of endeavour in vastly greater detail and illustrated with innumerable engravings had been John Britton and Edward William Brayley's *The Beauties of England and Wales*. This was started at the beginning of the nineteenth century and continued to come out in eighteen volumes all told over the years. When volume five appeared the authors announced that they had travelled over 3,500 miles. Frith's work however soon exceeded even theirs in scope. Derek Wilson, in his valuable biographical sketch of Frith, has remarked: 'His life spanned the whole Victorian era. He was born three years after Queen Victoria and died three years before her'. And during his repeated tours around the country, often with his family who referred to them as 'photo-tours', he came to know the spirit of those times and see its changes. In the surviving photographs it is quite common to see the same view taken three or more times over the decades and be able to plot change and development and, that most evanescent thing, 'atmosphere'.

Frith died in 1898 and many of the photographs, including some of those used here, were taken by young men that Frith had trained. We do not know their names but it is clear that, like the anonymous scribes and artists of the middle ages, they carried on working in the spirit and with the skills that they had been taught.

Why is 'Francis Frith's England' any different from the England portrayed by other photographers of the time? In photographing *everything* Frith made himself both a great observer and a great leveller. Other photographers took charming views of elegant watering-places and the fashionable resorts, and a selection of these narrower artists' work would show a narrower view of England. Fishing villages for example did not feature in a polite tour at all – too much hard work and smell of the sea! Selecting photographs from Frith's enormous output is made exceedingly difficult by this universal coverage but in the end the picture of the country which emerges is far more honest than that which could be made from any other photographer's work, and even in the small number which can be included in such a volume as this we are undoubtedly looking at 'Francis Frith's England', not anyone else's.

Our selection here begins with seaside England, something that every family knows today, but which only developed during the nineteenth century. This is followed by a look at that essential accompaniment of a seaside holiday, the paddle steamer, great numbers of which plied around the shores of the British Isles offering trips to holidaymakers. We then move to the most obvious thing to be seen from these cruises as they made their way around the coast – the countless small fishing villages, some beginning to use new methods and flourishing, others declining. Frith photographed every one of these and there is a rich selection to choose from. Even then there was one county whose fishing villages and fishermen marked themselves off from those elsewhere in the country, and we do the same here, giving an entire chapter to Cornwall. A brief look at two fundamental areas of the maritime world, life-saving and shipbuilding, is followed by what is effectively the second part of the book. This looks at the whole range of working maritime life, from the inland waterways down through the large rivers to the commercial ports that are the basis for many of England's great cities. The final chapter looks at those great institutions which have been, over the centuries, the machine which has driven the maritime world on – the navy and the commerce of England's great ports.

The majority of those visiting Britain would arrive through these ports and when they did most of them would already have a guide with which they were quite familiar – long sea voyages were ideal for reading. The one most commonly used was the ubiquitous Baedecker, and that is the one we use in the captions to the photographs.

It is interesting that all the photographs here could have been bought as single images by these visitors, although collections of them were sold in book form, just as Frith had done with his earliest photographs of Egypt and the Holy Land. There was no confusion then between the two arts of photography and literature and a fascination with photographs did not imply, as it well might today, semi-literacy on the part of the reader. The captions here serve instead of the Baedecker which the original purchaser would have had by him when he looked at the images, admiring them in their own right.

Frith's first tour of the country with his parents gave him a lasting interest in his own country. This interest was added to by his tours of Egypt which enabled him to see the wood, if England is a wood, from the trees: the masses of small detail in daily life in the innumerable villages, towns and cities in England and the countryside itself. His tours on the Continent enabled him to see afresh on his return those subtle characteristics of a maritime people which are not obvious to the people themselves but which, to someone who has been living on a continental landmass and never travelled overseas in that time, are striking. Although the motor car and air travel have lessened people's consciousness of their roots, they are nonetheless there still, and Francis Frith's Maritime England is as good a place as any to look for those which belong to England.

⊰ Chapter One ⊱
DAYS AT THE SEASIDE

During his long life Francis Frith watched the seashore change into the seaside. From being part of the country's working life, of interest to fishermen and few others, the seashore took on an entirely new role: that of provider of leisure and breathing space for people exhausted by their lives in the industrial and commercial centres of England. Most of these new watering-places, to give them their genteel title, had evolved from simple fishing villages. Some were favoured by visits from royalty in the eighteenth century and earlier; others became popular during the Napoleonic Wars when the aristocracy could not travel on the Continent quite as freely as they had been used to. Deprived of their Grand Tour they travelled about England – it is no coincidence that the word tourist appears at this time to describe such activities – and settled in places like Teignmouth and the newly expanding Torquay, both in Devon. A more interesting example is provided by Blackpool, which also began as a fishing village but was visited by members of the emergent business families of Manchester. With the coming of the railway this first trickle became a flood and the masters were soon followed by their workers on their days off. With ever-increasing speed Blackpool developed into what it is today, and the same process occurred all around the country.

There is one aspect of the seaside Frith has captured here which separates that world from ours and also gives his views a great deal of their charm, and that is the fashions. It is disconcerting to see in the photographs people who are better dressed for a day out on the beach than the average politician at an assembly of the United Nations. The women's fashions, particularly those from the Edwardian period, could not be in greater contrast to ours, while the men's clothes are recognizably those which today have formed the model for civilized tailoring all over the world, with the classic shirt, tie and suit, often three piece, and the more daring running to a blazer which evolved, with its cousin the hunting jacket, into modern versions loosely described as sports jackets.

The idea of bathing in the sea, which started early on and was seen as part of the way to regain health, only caught on in a general way very slowly and even then the bathing hut which could be seen everywhere at this time was always used. No matter how packed the beaches no one so much as took off their shoes, let alone any other item of clothing, unless they were first inside one.

The choice of the following photographs was influenced primarily by their photographic qualities, followed closely by those which show the regional differences which are now so rapidly disappearing, thanks largely to nationwide advertising and chainstores. We are moving today to the point where the only 'local' characteristics are the lie of the land and the actual appearance of the streets and the people themselves. All else is reduced to bland uniformity with multiple chains even breaking into the provision of local foods, so that a visitor to a Devon beach can be told by a seasonal worker that there are no such things as Devon pasties for sale – or known of – only pizzas. In Frith's day the people of, say, Bridlington would know that their town was different from any other and could point out just how and feel proud about it. In the same way these photographs capture the individual spirit of each seaside place before the uniformity brought about by a holiday industry really took root.

Eastbourne, East Sussex, at the height of the midsummer holiday season. Definitely one of the grander resorts with first-class hotels all along the front, grandly announcing that 'flys or omnibuses are sent to meet the principal trains'. The genteel tone can also be seen on the beach where, despite the massed ranks of the bathing machines receding into the distance, most seem happy to walk along in their most elegant town clothes. Even the boatmen pushing out the young couple in their rowing boat do not trouble to roll up their trousers or remove their shoes! The crowd gathered in the middle distance is too adult to be that around a punch and judy show; perhaps they are watching pierrots which performed at all resorts. On the horizon is the Martello tower known as the Wish, with its surrounding fortifications.

Flag-bedecked ships at the Dartmouth Regatta, South Devon, in 1886. Nothing epitomized elegant life afloat more than a regatta, with its origins in stories of the first great events on the Grand Canal in Venice brought back by wealthy families who had been on the 'Grand Tour'. Dartmouth Regatta held a special place in the annual calendar of every family who saw one of their sons through the naval college there.

The floating band playing beneath a string of Chinese lanterns bring a local touch of pomp and circumstance to the Fowey Regatta, Cornwall. Fowey is proud of its antecedents which go back well beyond those of its now more-famous neighbour Dartmouth. The barge in the middle distance provides a reminder that Fowey's river took commercial traffic, as it still does, but the families out on the water here listening to the band show an unusual side of late-Victorian social life.

This relaxed, uncrowded scene at Worthing, West Sussex, has in it all the elements of an old-fashioned day out at the seaside before sunbathing transformed the appearance of every beach. A contemporary guide refers to Worthing as a favourite watering-place 'frequented by those who like quieter quarters than Brighton'. Like so many other watering-places, it began its life as a fishing hamlet but the boost to its popularity came not from the Victorians but from a visit by Princess Amelia, the youngest daughter of King George III, at the end of the eighteenth century. Eight years before this photograph was taken Oscar Wilde was staying on the esplanade with his family while he wrote *The Importance of Being Earnest*. No doubt the play has been put on many times at theatres in the town or on the end of the long pier here. Frith's lens has caught here every detail of a typical afternoon: a couple being rowed around the shore, children in the water, daringly without their shoes, a steamer at the pier-head and a yacht going out for a cruise. There is even someone searching in the seaweed at the breakwater – perhaps for a fresh specimen.

The lifeboat at Newquay returning to a crowd on the beach showing intense interest and concern. We cannot know exactly what has been happening but there seems to have been a fortunate outcome as some people are walking away, and one holidaymaker is photographing the lifeboat, just as Frith is photographing the entire scene. In earlier days the lifeboat would have been out to rescue one of the fishing boats that went after the great shoals of pilchards that existed around the north cornish coast. In 1928, when this was taken, it would be far more likely to have been helping an amateur yachtsman in difficulties. The fishing fleet and the pilchards have gone, to be replaced by holidaymakers, many with an interest in surfing for which Newquay is renowned.

The shingle and sand beach at Southwold, Suffolk, at the mouth of the River Blyth. Nothing shows the contrast between then and now more than the white-bearded gentleman on the left with his family. Their deckchairs are identical to any that could be found on beaches around Britain today, but the people are unmistakeably late Victorian: a suit for the men, and full-length skirts and parasols for the ladies. Walking barefoot on the beach would have been a sign of one thing only – poverty! On the horizon can be seen the top of the lighthouse, which is actually in the town. The fishing boats in the foreground are marked LT for the nearby fishing port of Lowestoft.

Not everyone who went to the sea wanted to spend their time on crowded beaches, however elegant or fashionable the company. Llansteffan is a village in Dyfed, Wales, on the peninsula between the Rivers Taff and Towy. The scenery is magnificent, as can be seen here, looking across towards Ferryside.

In the sand can be seen the marks of carriages and horses that have passed while the tide was out. One of these appears to have gone out to where the boat is beached. An afternoon strolling along here beneath the trees with such a splendid view would make a refreshing contrast to the packed beaches of the more popular resorts. Llansteffan also featured a ruined Norman castle with gatehouse and keep. When the tide was in, a boat could be hired to take you over to Ferryside and to nearby Kidwelly which still has an immense medieval castle well worth exploring.

Gorleston Pier, Norfolk, taken in 1904. The ladies' elaborate walking dresses have not prevented them from making their way along this quite remarkable structure to find somewhere to sit and take in the sunshine and sea-air, whilst watching the fishing boats from Lowestoft down the coast going along the Yarmouth Roads, or waiting for the steamer, whose funnel is visible here, as it makes its way alongside. It is remarkable that, despite the strikingly photogenic quality of these old weathered timbers which are as noteworthy as any around the coast of England that Frith photographed on his journeys, Gorleston is not mentioned in Baedeker, or any of the main tourist guides. Even today it is not mentioned in either of the two most popular visitors' guidebooks, which perhaps accounts for the unspoilt elegance hinted at here.

Edwardian Eastbourne (East Sussex), on a chilly day, judging by the clothes. Although the fashionable women's hats and the boy's sailor suit suggest sophistication, a trip in a small fishing vessel such as this brought them into close contact with the sea in a way few now experience. The stupendous pier in the background is a classic with echoes of all kinds of architecture, British and colonial. Mock Tudor walls are crowned with roofs that would not have disgraced an Indian mogul's palace. The great two-storey pavilion at the end would have provided entertainment and refreshment for those awaiting the steamers plying between one seaside resort and the next.

Weston-Super-Mare, Avon, on the Bristol Channel is an example of the small fishing village with a few hundred souls transformed in the Victorian era into a flourishing resort for people from a nearby town, here Bristol. Baedeker's famous guide referred to Weston as 'a fashionable and well-sheltered watering-place – the bay affords abundant opportunity for rowing and sailing'. Frith's view here shows how accurate this brief description was, with sailing boats out on the water and passengers embarking at the water's edge, with other holiday-makers looking on. Everywhere the ladies carry parasols to protect them from the direct glare of the sun in an age when sunbathing was unheard of. Only one young man is wearing the more raffish blazer, whilst the vicar sitting on the rock in the foreground of the picture seems to be wearing a morning coat to go with his dog-collar.

30421. Fleetwood. F.F.& Cº.

Fleetwood in Lancashire, just up the coast from Blackpool. Writing about the time this photograph was taken, Baedeker remarks of it: 'A small watering-place and seaport on the Irish channel, with a good harbour. Mail-steamers ply daily hence to Belfast and there is a summer service to the Isle of Man'. The brick-built Customs Watch House, the elegant lighthouse, and the cannon lined up along the promenade all give the place a distinctive character. The children in the foreground, with more clustered on the roof of the Customs House outbuildings, seem to be on a school outing. The fisherman on the boat is attending to his sails, carrying on his work regardless of the chatter of the children about him. On one of the breakwaters in the distance an elderly couple sit beneath a parasol and watch the ships going in and out of the harbour many of which, in those days, used to be making for the waters of Iceland and Greenland. There is a complete absence of deckchairs or benches of any kind and one lady in the middle of the picture, perhaps a schoolmistress in charge of the children, is propped up against an upturned boat reading her book.

17

48499. Brighton; from West Pier. F.F.&Cº.

Brighton, East Sussex, originally Brighthelmstone, which was until the middle of the eighteenth century a fishing village like countless others around the coast. Then a doctor moved to the town and began to exhort people to visit saying they would find there 'sea air sea water and sea bathing' which together would act as a cure for all ailments. This idea points to the parallel between going to the seaside in England and the continental tradition of going to spas to take the waters. Brighton became unquestionably the grandest watering-place in the country with its Royal pavilion built by the Prince Regent, an extraordinary creation loosely based on an Indian maharajah's palace. When this photograph was taken the town was flourishing and had even acquired a somewhat risqué

reputation which led the more genteel to go further along the coast, or at least to its neighbour Hove.

The pier is refreshingly uncrowded. From the shadows it is quite late in the afternoon but the ladies in the centre still have their parasols up against the sun. The windows of the great hotels along the front are similarly sheltered by window awnings which nowadays have almost entirely gone. The small building beneath the flag on the left announces itself as a 'Camera Obscura' a sophisticated variation on the countless photographers' studios in the town which did a thriving business selling cartes-de-visite (small photographs mounted on cards) which visitors could send off to their relatives and friends as souvenirs of their visit.

Another pier, this time at Clacton, Essex, and taken from what seems to have been a first-floor hotel window giving an unusual perspective looking down the pier towards the two-storey rotunda at the end, but with all the detail at the front of the pier that the photographs usually miss. The timetable at the booking office gives the destinations Walton-on-the-Naze, Felixstowe, Harwich, Ipswich, Yarmouth, Southend, Gravesend and London with a timed service. Besides the paper shop and 'Little Cabin' for ices and teas there are baths providing hot and cold seawater for 'Gentlemen and Ladies' with the astonishing opening hours, for us today, of six in the morning to six at night. The idea of starting off on a steamboat excursion with a hot sea bath at six in the morning would seem quite mad today were it possible, but clearly the people of Clacton in 1907 must have used these services, for here they are.

Baedeker rather snootily remarks about Margate in Kent: 'One of the most popular, though not one of the most fashionable watering-places in England … On Saturdays and Sundays in the season both Margate and Ramsgate are uncomfortably crowded with excursionists from London brought in thousands by railway and steamer'. The selection of the 'thousands' seen here at the end of the jetty on a sunny afternoon waiting for the yacht *Sunbeam* to sail at three o'clock all seem quite presentable. True the yacht seems to be a rather rough and ready ketch, but this design was favoured by Charles II for his royal yachts, and it was he who first brought the word yacht into use in England in 1660. The fare for the trip, setting out at eleven in the morning and three in the afternoon is shown as one shilling for adults and sixpence for children, and very reasonable too. The table of destinations on the General Steam Navigation Co Ltd's building shows almost as many stops as on the railway line and marks the heyday of the use of steamers as ordinary transport. Only with the increasing congestion in London which has reduced traffic to slower speeds today than when horses were in use has river transport showed signs of coming back into favour.

Another magnificent Frith photograph which makes all description needless. The sea-worn timbers at the entrance to the little harbour of West Bay, Dorset, described in Hardy's Wessex novels as Port Bredy, are in perfect counterpoint to the grandeur of the cliffs going away towards Burton Bradstock and the famous Chesil Beach.

A still recognizable view of Torquay, South Devon. In fact the row of houses along the quayside has hardly changed at all today and the charming terrace of balconied houses rising up the hill is still there. What has changed is the sense of scale, and this has been caused by such things as the removal of the railings to the gardens, a change which occurred all over Britain in the great wartime scrap-metal drives, and the trees and hedges. The palm trees are still there but the rest of the trees and plants here have been trained almost to the standard of an ornamental garden. The trees along the roadside are still there, no doubt the same trees, but now of great height, largely obscuring the view. The sense of order and elegance embodied in the gentleman seated admiring the view here has all-but gone.

Torquay in 1904. Edwardian elegance can again be seen in the carefully tended trees, the elaborate rustic pavilion and the faultless lawn of the bowling green. All this has now been swept away and a yachting marina occupies approximately this spot. In the background in Torbay is the might of the fleet. People were very conscious of the navy at this time; Anglo-German rivalry was at its height and the importance of naval strength was made obvious to everyone by the Russo-Japanese war when Japan's fleet conquered Russia's with a navy that had been well equipped with battleships, constructed on Tyneside amongst other places. Today there are few such displays. Even one modern ship, a nuclear submarine armed with missiles, would have more fire-power than all the ships seen here, and so the whole matter is forgotten about and Torquay left to the tourists. The largest ships to leave the harbour in Torquay today are the ferries going to the Channel Islands, making an enjoyable journey for local people who do not want the bother of going to an airport upcountry and taking almost as long as by the traditional maritime route that starts on their doorstep.

Chapter Two

THE HEYDAY OF THE PADDLE STEAMER

Having fixed on their hotel or boarding house for their holiday, a family would explore the town and work out their daily promenade. If they returned year after year, as many did, they would get to know the various excursions taking a day – or two at the most. These could be to a neighbouring beauty spot, or the ruins of ancient abbey inland. But most constant favourite was a trip by paddle steamer from the pier. The coast of England was encircled by regular steamer services that took people from place to place, from resort to resort. There were many types of paddle steamer, such as the paddle tugs seen here at Scarborough and the paddle beam trawler. Commercially they were superseded by the more modern propeller-driven ship, but the type for long survived in the passenger paddle steamers which we see here.

Frith and his photographers were well aware of the peoples' fascination with the boats, and the part the local steam-packet company played in the economic life of the town. It was rare for them to photograph a pier without a paddle steamer at the end of it, either discharging passengers or pulling away with a fresh load.

A few steamers have survived to the present day – one on the Thames. They occasionally made more adventurous journeys, to the Isle of Man for example, or over to the Isle of Wight, but were most suited to taking people along the coast for a day's shopping or sightseeing. It is easy to forget in this jaded age that sightseeing meant what it said and a day's walk was considered admirably rewarded if some spectacular view could be found at the end of it. The weather was obviously a constant concern. Any journey afloat, however short, unless a mere rowing outing, raises the question of how good a sailor someone is. Rough weather could test the constitution of a city-dweller who had decided on a day at sea and found himself suddenly caught in a squall or heavy rain shower with the waves assuming mountainous proportions. But such problems were withstood in good spirits and could be talked about in the evening. A quick trip down the coast is now taken by car. The alternative is almost forgotten, as are the difficulties, the timetable, catching or missing a boat, and the sudden shock of the uncertainty and reality of going by sea rather than in a car along a motorway.

Frith's photographs of the boats are sometimes striking and often show their power, no matter how small they might be in actuality. Unfortunately taking a photograph aboard was technically impossible and would remain so almost until the ships themselves had ceased to play the part they did in his day.

The photographs are some of the best of their kind, but they are not the only record, and, as in all similar situations where the nature of a country's experience has changed, souvenirs and mementoes can be found all over the place. Family scrap albums contain postcards of the ships, even such ephemera as the tickets and brochures or a timetable can be found. As so often however, the essential things in people's lives are those most taken for granted and most difficult to find out about and there is little written history of the people in companies that managed these boats or the shipyards where they were built. Here we content ourselves with presenting this group of Frith's photographs of quite the most appealing part of maritime England on holiday.

Bournemouth, Dorset, and the paddle steamer Brodick Castle, here about to leave for Swanage. There were regular services in the summer to Poole, Portsmouth, the Isle of Wight and Weymouth as well. From Weymouth connection could be made for Lulworth Cove or Lyme Regis and so on in an extended coastal exploration that would now be made by car. The contrast between a day out on the sea and that of being confined in an enclosed space with the ever-present danger of accidents and only the company of a car-radio does not bear dwelling upon. One can only hope that sanity will finally prevail and the nation come to its senses! The passengers on this boat seem rather grand, and Bournemouth was soon to become known as 'The Queen of the South'. The tone of the place can be seen in a local guidebook which referred to the two piers as 'offering delightful opportunity for a marine promenade'. It went on to explain that Bournemouth owed its salubrity, a favourite Victorian word, to 'the luxuriant pine woods in which it is embosomed'. It was, in fact, a very pleasant place to stay.

The paddle steamer *Victoria* at Lulworth Cove, Dorset, in 1894. The grandeur of the Purbeck-stone cliffs encircling water that seems calm enough to be a lake has attracted visitors from the earliest days of tourism. There are dense crowds on board the ship in this picture and some can be seen alighting down a wheeled gangplank. Not everyone went ashore here but those who did often returned overland. They explored the cliff walks which extended for five miles of total isolation with great seas breaking against the limestone heights, including most famously an immense natural arch known as the Durdle Door to the west of this view. Despite the regular flow of visitors the local people still carried on their farming and fishing. Cattle may be seen on the hillside, and the nets and catch of a small fishing boat are laid out on the beach.

The paddle steamer *Prince of Wales* at Douglas, Isle of Man in 1907. Despite the fact that the arrival and departure of paddle steamers were the most prominent daily happenings in an island like the Isle of Man this boat still seems able to draw quite a crowd of interested spectators lining the hilltop, leaning against railings which must be singularly firmly fixed as there is a worrying sheer drop below. The elegant Edwardian fashions are again in evidence. The lighthouse and castellated keeper's house are striking. A closer look shows four builders hard at work, on traditional wooden scaffolding, building an additional range of buildings oblivious of the crowd on the hillside above them.

As with so many of Frith's most striking images he has achieved his effect by following the basic laws of composition and using a camera with great depth of field so that the people in the foreground are as sharply in focus as the boat hundreds of yards away.

This powerful photograph shows the paddle steamer *Alexandra* at Llandudno, Gwynedd. Llandudno, situated on the narrow peninsula between Conway Bay and Orme's Bay, is described in a contemporary guide as the most fashionable of the Welsh watering-places and one of the most attractive in the kingdom. It was also a major centre for steamer traffic, most of which was run by the Liverpool, Llandudno and Welsh Coast Steamboat Company. Their main service was a twice-daily trip between Liverpool and Menai Bridge calling at Llandudno, Beaumaris and Bangor. The steamers were fairly full most of the time and were packed, as we can see from these photographs, at the height of the season. The journey from Llandudno to Liverpool took two and three-quarter hours and cost four shillings and sixpence single and seven shillings return for first-class tickets, and two shillings and sixpence single, four shillings and sixpence return for second-class tickets. This works out at about twelve pounds return in today's terms for an ordinary return ticket for a three hour journey. The journey to Menai Bridge took one and a half hours and cost three shillings return or about eight pounds today. It is not hard to see why the trips were so popular. Modern visitor's guides to Britain do not usually mention the possibility of such journeys, but for any Victorian planning to stay somewhere for a holiday they would have been an essential consideration.

The *Alexandra* again, this time at Beaumaris, Anglesey, or possibly one of her sister ships on the line. The main reason for visiting Beaumaris, then as now, was the castle, which once had a seawater moat. The popularity of the steamer ride can be seen from the mass of people on the pier; it is so densely packed that some youths have climbed on top of the roof of the pier-cabin.

Another unusually attractive photograph, taken at Tenby, Dyfed. The slow film speed has given added charm by blurring into a pleasant meandering haze the smoke from the stack of the paddle steamer *Privateer*. The *Privateer* plied regularly in the summer to Bristol, Ilfracombe and Ilford, and the quay here is packed with people waiting to board. Tenby was also a fishing port, and those who wanted to go out in small boats could make use of the services of fishermen. They charged the princely sum of one shilling and sixpence per hour for a rowing boat with one man, or two shillings an hour for a sailing boat with two men. It is small wonder that the standard of living of the local fisherfolk was not high, although no doubt a tip would be expected.

The walls behind the quay here are part of the sixteenth-century fortifications against the armada. The local museum is described by Baedeker as containing relics of the last invasion of Britain carried out by a small force of French troops acting under an Irish-American officer which landed at Fishguard in 1797. Their original aim was the capture of Bristol!

The *Duchess of Devonshire* at the main pier by the entrance to Exmouth harbour in Devon. The timbers shown here only finally gave way in the 1980s although they had been much shored up and repaired meanwhile. Of the many small commercial ports around the coast Exmouth was one that flourished until very recently. Over half a million tons of cargo went through the port each year. The spectacle of ever-larger boats making their way with consummate skill into the exceedingly tight confines of the harbour was one of the things that fascinated holiday-makers and gave the town its own character, a character not so different from the one it had when this photograph was taken, nearly a hundred years before. The more genteel, who did not wish their eyes to be sullied by the sight of commercial activity, could go further along the coast to Budleigh Salterton or Sidmouth. Ironically today's city fathers of Exmouth are closing the port and building a marina in its place, with blocks of flats and town houses. A small port that has survived and flourished despite all the difficulties such businesses face in this century is to be closed, with great loss of jobs, to give the town that very gentility that the more robust members of the community have successfully fought against in an effort to keep the spirit of the town alive. In an age that supposedly looks back with pride to Victorian business spirit, a very un-Victorian outcome.

The romantic ivy-covered ruins of Pembroke Castle, Dyfed where Henry VII was born. The Victorians were quite happy to see their ruins clothed in ivy but the Frith archive has many series of photographs taken over the years well into the twentieth century which show the ivy being removed and the romantic ruins becoming clinical and institutionalized 'tourist attractions'. No doubt the removal of ivy did slow decay from one cause, although this is debatable. But the acid rain that then falls directly on to the stone does even more damage.

This view is particularly pleasing with the contrast between the castle and the paddle steamer in the foreground. Earlier captions to this photograph have referred to this as a passenger steamer one even giving a graphic account of its journeys around the coast crammed with tourists. But not all paddle steamers were passenger ships and this is a beam trawler, M20, converted from the steam tug *Flying Scotchman*. The beam of the trawl can clearly be seen. The fact that this is a working fishing boat does not detract in any way from the charm of the composition.

A small group of paddle steamers in Scarborough harbour, North Yorkshire, none of which ever had a passenger aboard it. The nearest,
Alexandra, is a paddle tug, the three others are beam trawlers called
Dandy (left) and *Constance* (centre), with the third unknown. The great
interest in the sailing fishing fleets has led people to forget the existence
of smoke-stained vessels such as these.

The shops on shore in the background are mercifully free of advertising which now dominates this and every seaside town. The only
lettering is that above the shops, one announcing that it is a ship's
tin-smith, another a rope store. The white building is the Bethel Mission
Chapel, appropriately enough next door to a public house and, towering
above the town along the hilltop is that remarkable structure which Frith
often photographed – Scarborough Castle.

Bridlington, Humberside, at its elegant and busiest, just before the outbreak of the First World War. Within a few years German battleships were to maraud down this coast, shelling towns as they went and the carefree atmosphere seen here went forever. A feature of this view, among the mass of activity, is the splendid brass telescope. Nowadays such an instrument would be immensely valuable and found in a museum, or anyway far away from the hands of any who simply wanted to part with a penny or two 'for a look'. The contrast with the modern coin-operated substitute shows that it is not only the standard of clothing that has fallen away since those days. Around the sundial a small group has gathered exchanging tales.

The paddle steamer boarding passengers in great number is the *Frenchman*. The fishing boats, characteristic of this part of the coast, seem also to be taking holiday-makers out, and between the sails on the left of the picture a yacht can be seen making its way out of the harbour.

⤙ Chapter Three ⤚
THE FRUITS OF THE SEA

Although most of the watering places visited by nineteenth century tourists had begun as fishing villages, by the time Frith came to photograph them much of their original character had gone. The smaller places or less desirable larger ports that had always been known as fishing ports carried on as they always had done, with fishing developing in some places and large new fleets, still mostly sailing ships, and new harbours. Other places kept up the original fishing techniques, particularly those who took lobsters and crabs. Large numbers of these places remote from railways carried on right into the twentieth century, when most were engulfed by the car-borne tide of tourists in search of the last 'unspoilt' spot.

Frith and his photographers captured with a unique thoroughness the life of these fishing communities as they went through slow processes of change, and were careful on the whole to take realistic photographs of what was going on. There was a strong tendency for photographers to find themselves taking what was essentially false, people posed in views which were deemed picturesque. This was particularly true of the villages which had been visited by colonies of artists. There are a few images in this chapter which show obvious sign of this kind of corruption: perhaps one of Frith's men succumbed to the temptation to produce a card that might 'sell'.

A sure sign of the confidence and simplicity with which Frith approached his work can be seen in the way people look at the camera with a curious self-consciousness. Even where the men have agreed to form a group and stand by their boats, or gather as a group, people can still be seen timidly looking from windows wondering what is going on.

It is commonplace today to bemoan the loss of these traditional fishing communities but it is in fact not always easy to say when a fishing village changes its character irrevocably, other than when the fishing stops and the people go over entirely to catering for tourists. Anyone looking at the few boats drawn up on Beer beach later in this chapter could not possibly think it could have survived, but it is still a thriving fishing village. St. Ives, on the other hand, once the rival of Newlyn as a fishing centre, has become simply a tourist resort with its original purpose only experienced through specially produced souvenirs.

Frith's careful study of every fishing village at many stages enables us to see the real world that these fisherfolk lived in. Although he did not set out to produce what might today be called a sociological or historical portrait of the places he visited, that is what he succeeded in doing. His pictures are filled with the detail which enables us to understand what fishing involved and what the places, boats and the people that lived out their lives working on the sea to provide food for their fellow countrymen were like.

Frith does not often give a title to his photographs beyond a simple name, but this one of Brixham trawlers he called aptly 'Waiting for a breeze'. When it was taken, in 1889, the trawling fleet at Brixham, Devon, was building up to its greatest strength, before the disaster of the First World War and the steady decline that followed, after a temporary revival in the post-war years. The fleet did not have a great history and was said to have been started by local businessmen when the merchant schooners that they funded for Newfoundland and other trades were supplanted by steam ships in the 1870s. The fleet also fulfilled a useful social func-tion, for the boys taken on in large numbers were frequently from local orphanages and homes. Brixham men fished all round England and were well known for finding new grounds, although the superior resources of the large east-coast fleets usually moved them on, in search of new grounds again. Surprisingly, in the 1970s and 1980s, there was a rapid revival in the fortunes of the fishing fleet, by this time equipped with motors and all the latest aids such as echo sounders. Sights such as these, however, have gone, never to be seen again.

Another fishing fleet, on the opposite coast of England, at Scarborough, North Yorkshire. Although to the layman's eye they seem much the same, a second glance will show that they are quite differently rigged, having two masts for example, and were sailed quite differently. The ship in the foreground, LT317 (LT stands for Lowestoft where these ships were registered), has a rowing boat with provisions alongside it, and sometimes part of a catch might be taken ashore in this way rather than the ship going into the dock. Frith took a sequence of photographs at this time showing horse-drawn carts lumbering out into quite deep water to meet these rowing boats, and sometimes the fishing boats themselves, and pick up the catch. The carts then took the fish back to shore where they unloaded them straight on to tables from where they were sold. Unfortunately the negatives appear to have been destroyed and the prints are only known from a single sequence at the Frith archive in Shaftesbury.

This photograph dates from 1890. A hundred years later fishing boats still go out from Scarborough though sail has given way to diesel.

A group of fishermen from Sheringham in Norfolk in 1908. Some of the earliest photographs known are of fishermen at Newhaven taken by David Octavius Hill and Robert Adamson in the 1840s. Despite the passage of sixty years there are strong resemblances. The candid and direct way the men look into the camera with their weather beaten faces is much the same, and the sea-boots and tar-stained clothes were as much part of being a fisherman in 1908 as in the 1840s.

In this photograph there are some signs of the twentieth century in that four of the men are wearing identical machine-made pullovers, of poor quality compared to those of half a century before. In an interesting example of oral history a visitor to the National Maritime Museum in 1978 was able to identify one of the men here – the one holding some line in his left hand – as a local character known as 'Go Far' Pegg who died about 1926.

Another group of Sheringham men repairing the characteristic local lobster pots in about 1906. They do not seem of the twentieth century either in their dress or in the way they look at the camera – in an entirely friendly and unposed way. A possible explanation for this is that Sher-ingham only became a holiday resort at the very end of the last century and they had had little time to become annoyed by photographers and the idle curiosity of strangers.

A cocklewoman at work on the warren opposite Exmouth, Devon, in 1906. This photograph is one of the most frequently reproduced of Frith's studies of local characters, and in recent years there has been a tendency for captions to point to the harsh life local people lived at this time, in shaming contrast to the elegant manners and dress of their Edwardian 'betters'. In fact they were part of a way of life which had no little dignity in a time of impending world conflict and the old lady here seems happy enough, just as are the people today who are carrying on this very simple tradition, although in Exmouth they are usually men. However no one is looking for cockles any more *exactly* where this woman is working because the land on which she is standing was washed away between the wars: in the sudden shifts of current and tide which can so frequently occur, the local inhabitants watched their warren, with summer chalets and cattle even, disappear over a period of only months. The mud is now a substantial spit of land extending from Dawlish Warren which only appears at low tide.

Behind the cocklewoman Exmouth Docks can clearly be seen, with the masts of a merchant schooner towering above the timber quays at the entrance.

When the fishing boats were out then only the women, children and the old men were to be found at home, as here at Llangwn, Wales. The old man's soft felt hat turned up at the brim and the woman's clothing are typically Welsh as are the young girls' charming good looks. The small boy on the right is touching his cap as he would have been taught to do as soon as he wore one, in a now forgotten gesture that shows the gulf separating this time from ours. His elaborate three-piece suit in what would be thought to be a poor fishing village contrasts with the t-shirt that a similar boy would be wearing today.

Two fishermen's cottages in a back alley in Tenby, Dyfed. The fishermen and boatmen of Tenby were notoriously badly paid in the days when fishing was a hard life at the best of times, and it is in places such as these that this is brought home to us. When people referred to these conditions and the lack of open views and fresh air it used to be jokingly said that fishermen saw enough of the sea during the day. The truth can be seen here in such details as the water-barrels at each doorway – running water would be unlikely in this simplest kind of dwelling – and in the absence even of windows, let alone a view. The girl furthest away from the camera is actually barefoot, a sure sign of absolute poverty in those days. Although there is anecdotal talk of children having no shoes being a fact of life in poor homes in Victorian England, this was actually very uncommon. In the many tens of thousands of Frith photographs taken in towns and villages all over the country such a thing is hardly ever seen. Even the child in arms in the last photograph for example, in a poor Welsh fishing village, has something on her feet. The Tenby of today has seen a total transformation and such conditions have long gone.

In contrast to the simple life at Tenby here are two fishermen's cottages at Whitby, North Yorkshire, known as Wilson's Yard, taken in 1913. As with similar courtyards in places as far away as Newlyn in Cornwall, the ground floors are reserved for the store of fishing gear and supplies and stairs lead up to what was in effect a flat or, as here, a maisonette (although it was not called that) where the fishermen lived.

Whitby had a photographer of its own who has become world famous, Frank Meadow Sutcliffe, and his photographs are indeed charming and show many facets of Whitby life. Frith could be said to be trespassing here, but in fact his simple topographical photograph taken without any of the atmospheric effects favoured by Sutcliffe still has considerable value as a record.

All working fishing boats have to be maintained continuously and Frith's photograph of Tenby shows two men hard at work on their trawler which has no doubt just arrived. They are in fact Brixham trawlers as can be seen from their markings and their rig, and these sometimes spent considerable time at places such as Tenby having come around the coast to fish in the Bristol Channel.

The young lad looking at the camera is the ship's boy, taken on as an apprentice and cook at two shillings per week all found. At seventeen after two years or so he would become third hand, then at nineteen would take his second-hand certificate, going on to become a skipper at twenty-one. The men on these boats needed to be fit and the average age of a skipper was about thirty; men of forty and over were rarely found on the boats.

Another, wider, view of the harbour at Tenby taken on the same day as the last photograph. The boat on the right is the ketch *Ann*. Nearly all the others are Brixham trawlers, making a fine sight closely banked together. At this distance, to the modern eye, they seem almost deserted. But a closer look shows the whole scene teaming with life, and most of the trawlers have their full crew aboard.

A general view of Whitby in 1880 with the foreground dominated by the topsail schooner *Astrea* built in 1826. Here again Frith uses one of his most effective compositional devices, placing an object of great detail and interest in the foreground as contrast to something of equal interest on the horizon and relying for his effect on the great depth of field of the lens he used. Here the ruins of Whitby are silhouetted on the hill above the town itself. Amongst the warehouses along the water's edge is one of particular interest. Its name can be read quite clearly on the original glass negative: 'William Harker's Jet Manufactory – Wholesale Ornament'. Jet, fossilized wood, was much admired by the Victorians and used for jewellery. It was found in great abundance in the cliffs near Whitby. It still occurs today, but the fashion and skills for working it are not the same. Whitby also had a considerable fishing fleet, out when this picture was taken, and of course a boatyard.

The fishing village of Staithes, North Yorkshire, entirely unspoilt and looking here, in the 1880s, much as it must have done for hundreds of years before. The fishing boats lined up at the end of the day seem as ageless and unchanging as the weathered striations on the cliffs beyond or the unaltered lives of the fisherfolk themselves. The men sitting on the foreshore mending their nets provide as great a contrast as possible with the fashionable tourists in the south coast resorts.

The rugged and picturesque quality of Staithes and its people at-tracted a number of artists earlier this century and helped create a new identity for the town with which it could fit into the twentieth century. Frith's photographs of the place recall an earlier age.

As with so many small fishing villages Staithes has its famous son: Captain James Cook started out here as a grocer's boy before running off to Whitby, and from there going on to sail the world and explore the southern seas.

Frith did not often take a photograph which highlighted social differences. This view taken in Staithes in 1932 is a rare example of the company breaking with tradition. The fishermen in their leather thigh-boots and sou'westers carrying a heavily laden barrel between them contrast starkly with the tourist whose only burden is a diminutive box-camera. His clothes are almost a living caricature of those that goaded George Orwell to some of his most furious outbursts and understandably so. One cannot imagine anyone in Edwardian England dressing this way, particularly the short trousers and absence of a hat – again in contrast to the fisherfolk. The Victorians would simply have burst out laughing at the spectacle.

But for the tourist's discordant presence, the view is typical of the simple unchanging environment in which people lived right through to the depression of the thirties when things became harder than they had ever been before. Only the cast-iron railings show any sign of even the Victorian era; the rest of the scene is timeless.

Gravesend, Kent, in July 1890. Here is another type of boat, immediately recognizable to fisherman of the time, called a bawley; there are four here and another beyond at anchor on the estuary. The men are undoubtedly the crew of one or other of the boats, but the young lady placed with her back to us is clearly someone who has agreed to pose for the photographer. Frith rarely posed people, and in fact this is one of the photographs in the National Maritime Museum's extensive collection not by Frith. The continuous river traffic which can be seen in the background has always been characteristic of the area, and the fact that fishing also went on just as it did in the remote villages of Cornwall and Yorkshire is often overlooked. These boats were used for coastal fishing and as oyster dredgers. Gravesend was also used in the seventeenth and eighteenth century as a port for journeys to and from the new world and has a particular claim to inclusion in the guidebooks, as the place where Pocohontas died. She is buried in the local church and in 1952 a Chapel of Unity was restored and opened to the public by Lady Nancy Astor in honour of the Indian princess.

Brixham harbour, South Devon, with the statue standing in an unfamiliar position for those who know Brixham today. The quay on this side has now been completely rebuilt running at the same height as that of the fish sheds in the background, and the statue placed on top of it. The local legend always had it that the statue was erected on the very spot where William of Orange was brought ashore on the back of a local sailor. From this view taken in 1897 it can immediately be seen that this was possible as there was no quay, instead a cobbled foreshore going down into the water.

The rise and fall and rise again of Brixham's fishing fleet has already been charted (page 36); this view shows Brixham booming as a fishing port, but before the influx of tourists and amateur painters. Hill's Commercial Inn still exists today but otherwise the entire town is packed with hotels and guesthouses and the popular entertainment industry that goes with them.

A strange effect here is the bright shaft of light that has caught the statue. The explanation of this is seen in the very next plate Frith took, included below.

Technical limitations normally prevented photographers of Frith's time from taking any interesting light effects, and it will have been noticed that without modern filters hardly any of Frith's images have noticeable clouds in them at all. This picture is a rare exception and a very dramatic one it is with the sun bursting through the storm clouds and being brilliantly reflected in the water and off the wet roofs of the fishermen's cottages. In the background on the quay the statue of William of Orange is just visible. The unusual light falling on it must have sent Frith running around the quay in order to see if he could capture the cloud effect that was causing it: as we can see he succeeded brilliantly.

The fishing village of Beer in Devon. This is one of the very few photographs in the Frith oeuvre taken from the water. The smallest fishing villages of this size are often those that are the first to go when the modern economic winds bring change, but the visitor to Beer today would find the appearance of the village largely unchanged and boats still there drawn up on the shore, but with engines, radar and every other modern device that fishing needs to stay competitive and alive. Why this should be so only the local fishermen whose forebears owned these boats could tell you.

Beer was famous at this time for its lace, much of which was taken to Honiton to be sold and hence known as Honiton lace. Local people claim that the finest Victorian Honiton lace, including Queen Victoria's famous christening gown, was all made by Beer women and girls.

Lympstone on the River Exe in Devon, and in all essentials the view from this spot today, nearly a hundred years later, has hardly altered. The clock tower, Peter's Tower, is still there and still being mistaken by visitors for a church; it was actually put there by the local landowner a few years before this was taken in memory of his wife and the care she had taken for the poor families in the village. All the other buildings remain unchanged as well except that the warehouses and commercial buildings along the shore have all been converted into cottages with windows looking out over the estuary. The foreground of the picture with nets just visible has been concreted over and is used as hard-standing for the boats of the local sailing club. This has meant the loss, except for those of a few hardy souls, of the local fishing boats. The poles are still there, but very few nets, although the spirit of the village has lingered on and made it one of the most sought-after retreats on the estuary.

Hallsands in Start Bay, Devon, and from time immemorial the source of some of the best crabs to be had in England. Apart from the stunning beauty of the coastline and the almost miraculous sense of isolation from the turmoil of the twentieth century – the picture was taken in 1924 – the photograph also shows us a self-contained fishing community that survived until the last few years from crab fishing alone using the old local methods and fishing straight off the shore without harbour or shelter.

On the beach are the boats and the local crab pots. These were all made by the men themselves from willow grown in small areas locally from time out of mind simply to fill this need. The bait for the crabs was caught in seine nets and then salted and dried. It can be seen here drying, some on the beach just to the right behind the man and two youths on the ruined wall, some on the beach behind the boats. The best account of these men and their lives and skills was made by an American professor, Melvin Firestone of Arizona State University, who visited the fishery in 1974-5. But visions of perfection can often conceal tragedy, and this one sadly is no exception. Firstly, in the winter storms of 1903-4 much of Old Hallsands was destroyed; secondly, during the Second World War many hundreds of young American servicemen lost their lives at Slapton Sands in the bay in a bungled attempt to simulate the proposed Normandy landings. The local people lived with their knowledge of the tragedy which was denied by the authorities until the late nineteen-eighties, when a shame-faced admission was made.

The view here is still beautiful.

Hope Cove, Devon, on a hot summer's day with the sun almost overhead as we can see from the deeply etched shadows on the path. The postman was a vital link for all villages and people in country places throughout the Victorian era, from the time of invention of the penny post until the telephone. In 1926 when this photograph was taken local people knew of the phone but would not have one in their homes; the local gibe was 'Phones are for people too lazy to go down to the phone box'. Hope is a small village halfway between Hallsands and Plymouth. The doldrums that afflicted the fishing industry affected Hope as well but the local economy has been maintained through the century by the continuous stream of tourists and people buying second homes there, attracted by its superb location.

The best of the guides to contemporary Britain describes Clovelly in North Devon as 'One of the show-places not only of Devon but of Britain. Cars cannot enter the village and the cottages lining the steep main street are decked with flowers for most of the year. The village lies in a lush narrow combe between steep cliffs'. All quite true and a pointer to the reason why the failure of the fishing industry has had little effect on the local economy. When this view was taken, in the 1890s, the beauty of the place was already such that painters were drawn to it – there is one here on the quay on the right under his umbrella. He seems to be a professional as he is working in oils rather than an amateur's watercolour. One wonders if he included Frith and his camera in his study.

The considerable number of boats in what is, perhaps, only a small harbour show that fishing was still going on, but its great days had been in Elizabethan times when an eminent lawyer George Carey thought it worth while building this quay entirely at his own expense.

❧ Chapter Four ❧
CORNWALL

The fishing villages of Cornwall have long been recognized as having qualities that are to be found nowhere else. This was partly because of their remoteness, which left old traditions intact long after they had largely disappeared in other parts of the country, and partly because of the strong light and temperate climate. The local buildings, whitewashed cottages in narrow lanes and courtyards, had more than a passing resemblance to fishing ports in the Mediterranean.

But there were other qualities, which were to be found in the people themselves. A classic example of this was provided by the famous Newlyn riots, said to be the last time in Britain that troops had to be sent to put down an open insurrection, backed up by warships standing to offshore. The cause of this remarkable incident in 1897 was the arrival in Cornish waters of fishing boats from the east coast, referred to as yorkies, whose boats were owned by companies which worked on strict principles of economy. This meant in real terms that they fished on Sundays, an unthinkable thing to the God-fearing chapel-going communities of Newlyn.

A tense situation finally erupted when one Sunday some Lowestoft boats had arrived with their usual load of pilchards. The Newlyn men threw hundreds of thousands of the fish into the sea in a pitched battle which has not a few resemblances to the 'Boston Tea Party', and the authorities were called in to deal with matters. In those days there were few police in Cornwall and troops had finally to be called. Unlike its Boston precedent, the Newlyn insurrection was suppressed and the leaders ended up in court. Contrary to our images of Victorian ruthlessness in such matters – in reality a modern phenomenon reflecting the tensions in a society beset by global conflicts – the men were let off very lightly. The root causes of their behaviour had been too serious and the whole affair was seen in a political light. Today there are interesting echoes in other parts of the world of disturbance with a religious base, and one can only admire the Victorian administrators for the wisdom which they brought to their task.

The Newlyn men were not however typical of the entire Cornish community. Indeed, while some villagers supported them, others a short way up the road in Penzance took a very different view and were happy to have Lowestoft boats in their harbour. But the native characteristics are nonetheless there. They can be seen in these photographs of Frith's which provide us with a genuine glimpse of that world.

Newlyn Court, Newlyn, known as Jenny Lind Court to the photographers who would invariably go to photograph it when they wanted an image that would make a perfect souvenir photograph for visitors. Some have thought because of this that such pictures were posed and unreal, but *Jenny Lind* was real enough. She was a first-class lugger and was actually broken up in the year this photograph was taken, 1906. The ship's dinghy is here for the very good reason that the gentleman in the bowler hat owned the boat.

These courtyards bear a strong resemblance to the courts we have seen at Whitby with flats above sheds, although here the stores have been moved to the end. The majority of courts at Newlyn have the whitewashed walls characteristic of Cornwall and they were always cobbled like this one. Today all the courts with cobbled yards have gone. Fishing in Newlyn was thriving at the turn of the century; a new harbour had been opened in 1894 and landings had increased immensely between then and the time this picture was taken.

The open fish market at Newlyn, taken on the same day as the last photograph. The woman on the left of the picture is carrying a fish-wife's cowl, a basket which was used either to carry pilchards up from the beach to the pilchard cellars or, as here, to hawk them. Frith has been accused of dishonesty in his photographs of women wearing cowls, attempting to portray a life of hardship long gone even in his time. But this photograph gives the lie to that idea. The woman is clearly using the cowl in her normal way of business and is obviously looking at her bill from the market to check what she has just bought. The photograph is quite 'real' and unposed. The fishermen in calf-length leather boots and the boy in the background in white blouse and knee-breeches gives the picture a European, almost Slavonic air. But in fact the people are simply reflecting the very strong local culture amongst the Newlyn fisherfolk. It was this that drew a colony of artists to Newlyn at the turn of the century and produced some of the most authentic British painting of the day. The romantic aura, if one was looked for, no doubt came from rumours of the Newlyn riots.

Newlyn's covered fish quay in 1908 showing clearly the scale of its fishing business – the picturesque luggers have gone never to return. Although there were to be great fluctuations in catches and changes in the fish stocks – the disappearance of herring between the wars, the sudden resurgence of mackerel in the late sixties – confidence and investment in the industry has been maintained. Newlyn is now said to be the fourth largest fishing port in the country exceeding Hull, North Shields, Lowestoft and Fleetwood.

Newlyn Harbour in about 1920 when the post-war crash – the Newlyn Pier and Harbour Commissioners reported fish landed in 1918 as a fifth the 1910 figure – had given way to a sudden boom. In 1920 the value landed was £274,387 compared to £109,548 in 1910.

The World War has made little difference to the atmosphere here. There is a domestic scale to the scene and those gathered around are not tourists but local people for whom the quality and quantity of a catch was a matter of some judgement. The man on the right is a builder's labourer, a plasterer from the trowel he is carrying, but his interest is as keen as everyone else's on the quay. The more so perhaps because this is a St. Ives boat.

When people think of a Cornish fishing village the name St. Ives is always the first to spring to mind. Generations of visitors all looking for a typically 'unspoilt' fishing scene have taken their toll and now the fishing industry has almost gone and the whole town is turned over to tourism.

Here, in a typical Frith photograph of about 1890, we can capture some of the atmosphere that originally gave St Ives its fame. The fishing boats are out at sea and chickens are wandering over the sands. Small children have been left in a convenient boat to keep them out of trouble while older ones run about appearing as 'ghosts' on the print, no doubt to the photographer's annoyance. The ship masts lying at random on the sand and the cascade of slate roofs over granite buildings that seem to grow out of the rock are St Ives and nowhere else.

A cobbled courtyard in St Ives showing again the characteristic store room on the ground floor with steps up to the first floor where the family lived. Both the cottage on the right and the one further back on the left have their occupants, elderly fish-wives, looking out at the photographer, one from her doorway, the other from her window. But the other figures here clearly do not belong to the scene. In 1906, when this was taken, there is already a conscious attempt to recapture the atmosphere seen in the last photograph. The placing of the youth, his shoes removed for the purpose, and of the young girl who actually looks acutely self-conscious, is the sort of thing that Frith himself never stooped to. Although one of the rare breaks with Frith's tradition, the picture itself no doubt proved very popular.

A general view of St Ives harbour with pilchard boats just in, before the nets had been cleared. The harbour beyond shows little change in 1908 from the view in 1890 (page 62), with some masts still to be seen on the beach and ships being repaired there. A close look at the shop in the background however shows small children peering into the window which is covered with the first wave of mass advertising, for Fry's Cocoa.

For the rest the scene is still unspoilt. In a slightly unusual detail which photographs will sometimes reveal, the boat on the right, although a St Ives boat, can be seen to have a sail from a Penzance-registered boat. No doubt the friendly rivalry between the two places did not go so far as refusing to help out a man from around the coast who had lost his sail.

Mevagissey now rivals St Ives as a mecca for the tourists. Today the flow of cars in the height of the season frequently leads to the closing of the town to them entirely. Here we see Mevagissey in 1890 at the height of its days as a fishing port, with the fishing fleet in. A group of ships' boys have gathered together in the sun on the rock and an upturned boat in the foreground. The fishing boats are dwarfed by the great ship alongside them which is identified by the National Maritime Museum as the schooner *Marshall Keith*.

Mevagissey harbour from another viewpoint, and forty years later. Improvements in film quality over the intervening years mean that we can now see the gulls wheeling over the boats. They would have been present in even greater numbers in the last photograph but the film and camera speeds available then meant that they were moving too fast to be captured although occasionally one can be seen at rest. However even the gulls cannot conceal the fact that the intervening forty years had seen the backbone of the industry broken. The single motorcar on the quay, its owner taking a photograph with his 'box-brownie', is a harbinger, while the few old-fashioned open trucks show only too clearly that there was little doing in the way of business. The post-war years were to see the harbour filled with boats again, but this time nearly all belonging to amateur sailors, or people with a weekend or summer cottage there, now priced well out of reach of the young fishermen just married who would have occupied them in years gone by.

The first in a fascinating series of photographs that shows the scene on the quays at West Looe just after the boats have come in with their catch on a fine day in 1889. Because Frith numbered every plate that he took and kept meticulous records we can often follow his exact sequence of movements as he set about capturing the spirit of the scene in front of him – there has been an earlier example of this at Brixham (pages 36 and 50). Here, in number 21309, we have the men gathered around, no doubt waiting to hear what the result of the fishing has been, so that they can be paid off for the day. The fish themselves have already been taken from the boats and are being sorted and cleaned immediately. This is Frith's next image.

Here young women are cleaning the fish that have just come from the great mass of netting piled up behind them. The intrusion of the modern world can be confined to the prosaic metal bucket they are using for scraps. The fish themselves are going from the wicker baskets into the traditional pottery vessels. This negative, meticulously numbered in the plate, was 21310. From here Frith walked past the women and around the corner to get a better view of the sweep of the harbour wall along the river bank of West Looe, a most charming and photogenic scene.

Here is number 21311, the last photograph in the series – all taken on five-inch by four-inch glass negatives. We see a boat from which the fish have been taken and the wicker baskets are back on deck empty. The woman in the foreground is no doubt cleaning the utensils she has been using. The black line running along the top of the wall in the distance as far as the eye can see is not a hedge as might be thought at first glance but row upon row of nets hung up to dry.

Although Looe has been swamped with tourists in recent years, like everywhere else in Cornwall, fishing still continues, and it has become a centre for shark fishing which would have come as no little surprise to the men who sailed the boats seen here.

Another scene at Looe but, surprisingly, taken over twenty years after the last sequence, in 1912. It is a little further around from the scene with the young fisherwomen cleaning fish, but the pattern of life has not changed at all. The wagons are still drawn up outside the warehouse, even the ropes are put down at exactly the same place on the quayside. The boat at the quay is a merchant schooner this time, and the photograph is made once again by the two young children in the foreground in traditional clothes, entirely unposed, waiting to be taken across the river to East Looe.

This marvellously evocative picture of life in a fishing village, Polperro in Cornwall, taken in 1889, shows a world that was soon to vanish. The scales weighing the fish in the centre of the picture were no doubt exactly similar to scales used centuries before and, except for the clothes which can be dated by the hats to the nineteenth century, nothing in the photograph would have been in the slightest bit different a hundred years earlier. The ground is simply the mud of the foreshore with no sign of tarmac or even cobbles or stone. Since most of the inhabitants would have been unable to read or write there was no need for advertising or garish shop-fronts. It is small wonder that artists looking for some release from the increasing pressures of urban life came to such places as Polperro, which captured this bygone world even more than St Ives. Here again we see the classic pattern of a house with storage on the ground floor with the house above it although, as is to be expected, with local variations in the architecture.

Mousehole in 1892. The fishermen here distinguished themselves by siding with the Newlyn men in 1897 in their brush with authority, sticking to their traditional chapel ways and refusing to fish on Sundays. Things are calm here now and there is no sign of these stirring events only a few years off. Men examine a boat to see exactly what repair work needs to be done and on the far side of the quay a few men are at work. But the only sign of the flourishing fishing trade is the masses of nets which literally carpet the quay in the foreground and stretch right around the far wall where they hang in great swathes as they dry in the sun.

Sennen Cove, just short of Land's End, and the westernmost village in the country. The old sailor and the thatched cottages in the middle distance suggest a Victorian photograph, but in fact this was taken in 1928. The round house on the right performed a double function: below was a capstan house, perhaps the machinery in the front has come from it, whilst the upper part acted as a net loft.

Buildings of this kind are a delight to those who admire traditional forms, methods and materials where the form of the building reflects its function. This building is in stark contrast to the modern concrete and steel buildings which dominate our cities and the only time that form reflects function is when computers needed in the offices require special depth in the floor space to accommodate their cabling.

The only cabling to be seen here is that made of strong hessian used for the traditional purpose of pulling boats up on to the shore.

⊰ Chapter Five ⊱
THE PERILS OF THE DEEP

Danger transcends all differences of class and background, and all differences across time as well. None are more aware of this than the fishermen and others who, on a voluntary basis, supported only by public appeals, come forward to man the lifeboats. Maroons or some other more traditional warning would announce that a ship was in distress and the local people would go and watch the launch of the boat, sometimes helping to pull it down to the shore.

The public feeling when the crew of a lifeboat is lost trying to save lives is still one of the most powerful that can grip the country. The outpouring of sympathy and assistance that flowed when the Penlee lifeboat was sunk and the crew lost their lives was as strong in modern Britain as that which spread through communities in Victorian times when lifeboats went down.

Today The Royal National Lifeboat Institution, or RNLI, is among the most popular charities in the country. Founded in 1824 as the Royal National Institution for the Preservation of Life from Shipwreck, the RNLI maintains all the lifeboat stations in Britain and is involved in continuing research into the latest advances in construction, electronic navigation and every other aspect of life-saving, most recently including helicopters as well.

Frith's photographers inevitably came across the RNLI, both its crews and its boats, and also the monuments to ships saved and people whose lives had been lost. Some of the most striking images have been brought together here.

The lifeboat memorial at Lytham St Anne's, Lancashire. The crew of the St Anne's lifeboat lost their lives in a gallant attempt to rescue the crew of the German barque *Mexico* in December 1886. This photograph was taken in 1894, a few years after the memorial's erection. Then, as now, the tragedy of men losing their lives to save others at sea strikes a unique chord in the national consciousness; putting up a statue was a typical Victorian response. Today the response would be more financial, in order to provide security for the relatives; a realist sculpture like this, or the sculptor to make it, would be difficult to find. The collecting box in the pillar is for the Royal National Lifeboat Institution.

38419 Skegness "Lifeboat." F.F&Co.

One of the most popular advertising posters for a seaside resort ever produced, painted by the gifted artist John Hassal, showed a cherubic laughing sailor skipping delightedly along the beach at Skegness in Lincolnshire with the slogan 'Skegness is so bracing'. This photograph shows another side to Skegness. The jackets seem quaint to us now, and the immaculately painted lifeboat seems almost like a showpiece. But one look at the faces of the men shows how seriously they carried out their duties and how important they and their boat were to those whose lives depended on them.

All the elements of the lifeboat tradition can be seen here at Great Yarmouth, Norfolk. The vertical board on the left records the lives saved by three successive Great Yarmouth lifeboats, including the *John Burch*. Pasted below the painted tributes is a poster advertising the town's 'Lifeboat Thursday' for 5 August 1896 which all interested were invited to attend. The model lifeboat is a small collecting box for the RNLI, many of which still exist, and it epitomizes the Victorian tradition of voluntary service and donation where the state plays no part which has survived right through to the present day. Hung along the walls are the harnesses for horses to pull the boat down to the shore, and the cumbersome lifejackets worn by the men. An unusual feature of this boat is the early form of wheel made from hinged flat plates of steel – later to see its ultimate development during the First World War as the basis for tracks used on tanks, for the taking of lives rather than the saving of them. The noticeboard carries a stern warning to the public not to touch the lifeboat 'or any of its gear' and the old sailor putting his faith in the stout timbers of the boat ensured that the public could look but not touch, nd that the boat was indeed ready at all times.

Apart from stability and a crew that could be aboard their boat with the greatest possible speed, the main factor that designers worked on was the best method to get the boat launched in the fastest time. The solution for each place was different and depended entirely on the topography of the coastline at that point. One method often used is seen here at Broadstairs, Kent, an old Regency watering-place that was later made famous by Charles Dickens who wrote *David Copperfield* here, and whose 'Bleak House' now contains a Dickens museum.

On the cliffs nearby is a lighthouse that gave bearings to shipping in the Thames estuary. It must have been of some comfort to those afloat to know that there was a lifeboat on shore as well.

Once again Frith has captured many different facets of a place in one image: the lifeboat and dark old timbers with the sea crashing against them show one side, the elegant Regency terrace in the background with elaborate wrought-iron balconies above bow-fronted windows at street level, another.

⊰ Chapter Six ⊱
SHIPBUILDING

Like all basic crafts, shipbuilding was originally intimately associated with the communities it served. The boats were built and repaired within the communities that used them. With industrialization, however, came steam power and the use of metal and these necessitated more remote and ever-larger yards. Nevertheless in the Victorian era the old link between the shipbuilders, especially those building sailing ships, and the people that used the boats was not entirely severed. A famous modern television series that has done more to popularize sailing clubs than any other is set in a shipbuilding yard where old-fashioned materials and design cling on against the ever-greater inroads of fibreglass and other more sophisticated modern materials; but this yard is concerned almost entirely with sailing yachts, not commercial boats, and the links with any working community are slight.

Frith and his photographers were not conscious of the interest that shipbuilding would have for a later generation. He took it for granted that shipbuilders were always to be found, large and small, much as other trades were to be found, and did not go out of his way to find them or photograph them. It is all the more interesting therefore to find in odd corners of Frith's negatives a boat being constructed or repaired. In one case the ship is prominent on the horizon, in others it has to be looked for. But the interest in them when found is great. It is as if alongside an ancient cathedral the original stonemason was found still at work with a continuous tradition going back to when the buildings were originally constructed.

In the case of the merchant schooners the origin of the design of these vitally important boats is shrouded in mystery. The rigging, the profile of the hulls, the construction are hardly ever written down, as Basil Greenhill's remarkable book *Merchant Schooners* makes plain.

The photographs here are augmented with a few from other photographers, to compensate for what was, clearly, a lack of interest on Frith's part. That lack of interest was only a reflection of lack of interest on the part of the general public who, again, although they may have turned out in great numbers for the launch of such ships as Brunel's *Great Eastern* would no more think of going to look at an ordinary shipyard at work than a modern motorist would think of going to see his car being made, or even going into his garage to see it being repaired or overhauled. Then as now the amenities of life are taken for granted.

Bridgwater, Somerset, on the River Parrett, taken towards the end of last century. In its day, until it was overtaken by Bristol, Bridgwater flourished and was an important port. The atmosphere here evokes that of an earlier age and has more of the 1830s about it than the 1890s. In the centre of the picture a ketch the *Gloster Packet* is undergoing repair on an impromptu drydock built on the river bed.

The traditions of shipbuilding here surviving were as ancient as the port itself and of considerable consequence for America in its earliest days: the *Virginia* of Sagadohock, said to be the first Old-World ship constructed in America, was built by George Popham who was born here. He and his brother Sir John Popham were pioneers of exploration in Maine, and there was even a short-lived settlement named after them on the Kennebec River there. Frith has captured in his lens actual evidence of the roots of American shipbuilding, showing it still being carried on where it had begun hundreds of years before.

The River Ouse at Selby, North Yorkshire. Here we see again the native shipbuilding tradition but in a different part of the country. This view is taken in 1901, a little later than the view of Bridgwater. The boat owners are clearly making a stab at taking on the new century and the new trades. Besides the ship in the background being constructed in the time-honoured way they have two steam ships, the *Mabel* and *Carlyle*, in for repair. Despite these efforts the atmosphere is still that of rural England and the landscape on the opposite bank looks more permanent than the dockyard.

Selby also has considerable interest for American visitors to England as one of the branches of George Washington's family lived nearby and in the magnificent abbey, restored since Frith's day, are stained-glass windows with the family crest showing the earliest representation of the stars and stripes known in England.

A thriving scene on the River Tamar that divides Devon from Cornwall with the viaduct at Calstock rapidly approaching completion. This stretch of the river was a favourite excursion from Plymouth on paddle steamers as far as Weirhead, and then, as Baedecker remarked 'there is much fine river scenery further on which may be visited by small boat'. Today tourism is the main activity here and the promise of change and growth that seems so strong in this picture came to nothing.

The principal interest of the scene for us is the signs beneath the viaduct of the ancient native life of the river such as the boatyard on the bank where a sailing barge is under construction. The main cargoes carried by these boats were granite, lead and other ores from the local mines. The tradition flourished from the earliest days until the beginning of this century and the ship being built here could well have been one of the last. The maritime historian Basil Greenhill has referred to Calstock as 'a perfect example of maritime decay ...' There are signs of vanished industry and former seaborne trade everywhere, but Calstock has turned its back upon the water and many of its people do not know that ships and maritime trade were once part of its life. In truth Calstock is not alone in experiencing such change, as we have seen elsewhere, but this photograph is a particularly poignant historical record of profound change at the roots of the local economy.

The River Wye and the ancient town of Chepstow, Gwent, the lowest crossing of the river, dominated by the rugged grandeur of Chepstow Castle. Of Norman origin with many thirteenth and fourteenth century additions, the castle has held some important prisoners in its time such as the regicide Jeremy Taylor. Its main interest now is to tourists who flock to the town which is extremely picturesque and still largely unchanged from the view seen here. The charming bridge with its delicate unequal arches designed by John Rennie is still in good order, although a startling modern road bridge has been built at exactly the spot from which this photograph was taken. The main change that has taken place is in the life along the river bank.

Once again a native tradition integral to the place since its foundation can be seen still carried on here in 1906. A small boat is clinging to the steep mud river bank, with men at work on her from the shipyard above. Slightly to the left the parallel lines of a rudimentary slipway can be followed back across the road to a ship either under construction or undergoing extensive repair. The sheeting put up to shield the boat from the weather has just caught the sunlight.

As in places such as the fishing village of Lympstone in Devon, today all the warehouses have long since been turned into houses or cottages and it is doubtful if their present occupants know they are living in what was once home to a thriving local industry.

The fishing port of Brixham, South Devon, in 1897. Here Frith has taken an unusual view of the town which is interesting to us now in showing not just the picturesque fishing boats under sail and the narrow streets but the other side of maritime life we have been looking at here, the repair and construction of the boats themselves. In the foreground two boats are in course of construction. The nearest one has just been laid down and only a few ribs can be seen, the one next to it is far advanced. Beyond are small yards with masses of every kind of timber likely to be required.

As with so many of Frith's photographs, to modern eyes it seems as though he has chosen either a Sunday or a quiet time of day to take his photograph. But in fact there are people at work here who can be made out by looking closely. Four men are working on the deck of the ship nearing completion. The diagonal timber in the small yard beyond them is in fact the arm of a wooden crane and the white sleeves of the man operating it can just be seen. Similarly men are at work on the quay and in the boats.

We are so used to an age of cars and large numbers of people walking about any picturesque place such as this, that a time when the only people in sight would be people at work is hardly imaginable. We assume the scene is deserted and look no further.

Uncommon among Frith's photographs and a yawning gap in the great photographic collections made in Victorian times are photographs such as this which show building work going on. Frith has hundreds of photographs of docks large and small, but this one of a new dock at Charlestown, is unique. No doubt it was included simply because it happened to be there when the photograph was taken, although it could have been the reason for a different 'prettier' view to be chosen. Luckily Frith resisted the temptation and we have this interesting picture.

The cranes are all of timber, but the industrial age has not been entirely neglected and can be seen in the steam engine on the left with a large wheel and immensely long belt most probably driving the chains of the main crane through gearing via a clutch. There are about twenty men at work here all expert at moving the great timbers and granite blocks that are going to make up Charlestown's new quay and dock.

The Victorians excelled at massive works such as this, whether highly visible or less obvious achievements such as the great underground hygienic systems in our great cities which after a hundred or more years we are now finding need renewal. The skills and crafts then used are having to be rediscovered but using new materials and modern machinery.

From the smaller fishing-village boatyards to the great yards making ocean-going ships and battleships is a great leap, but the traditions and crafts are related to each other in an unbroken progression. The scene here is the launching of the *Sans Pareil* on the Thames in 1887. She had been built by Thames Iron Works, Blackwall. The scene is one of great elation and enthusiasm which strongly resembles a regatta, with members of the shipwrights' families coming down to see the great event. People are crowded on the dockside or peering eagerly from boats being rowed as hard as they can to keep up with the ship as the tugs pull her into midstream. Those taking part remembered these occasions as highlights of their lives for years to come. The nearest equivalent ceremony today has been, perhaps, the royal opening of the Thames flood barrier. There is a great deal of construction work going on in Thames docks today but it is almost entirely office blocks and houses. These are being built over what was once one of the busiest ports in the world: the last thirty years have seen the almost impossible happen. Before their eyes, and the eyes of astonished Londoners for whom the river and its shipping were part of the unchanging order of things, the trade went. The docks closed, except for Tilbury and other isolated areas. New technology arrived using containers and the ever-more popular roll-on, roll-off ships, but the dockers, largely under Communist leadership, would not or could not accept the new world of working practices that this implied. The news was not all bad, however, for new docks such as Felixstowe specializing in the new technology have sprung up to take the business that London did not want.

An awe-inspiring sight, the SS *Aquitania* nearing completion at John Brown's shipyard on Clydebank in 1913. Apart from the enormous scale, seen by comparison with the figure on the bank on the left looking up at the ship, the most striking thing to modern eyes is the forest, almost literally, of timber scaffolding – in the days when tubular-steel scaffolding poles were unknown. That such a perfectly engineered object should appear from the midst of what seems totally unscientific confusion amazes us, we who are used to the neat right angles and rigorous safety regulations of the modern age.

John Brown and Co, a Sheffield firm, acquired the shipyard at Clydebank, Strathclyde, which had sprung from nothing in thirty years, at the very end of the nineteenth century. The ships which followed the *Aquitania* in an ever more distinguished line included the *Lusitania*, *Queen Mary*, *Queen Elizabeth* and *QE2*.

⊰ Chapter Seven ⊱
FROM THE LAND TO THE SEA

The first great revolution in British transport was that created by the canals. But these were simply extending and developing the advantages of the natural waterways which determine the face of England and the location of every town, city and village in the country.

The greatest canal of all the Manchester Ship Canal was only built late in the nineteenth century when the other canals had largely fallen into disuse. It is perhaps for this reason that Frith does not seem to have paid great attention to canals as such; the famous flights of locks he notices, and picturesque byways, some of which we see here, but for the rest he was more concerned with natural beauties, such as the Norfolk broads, and the way of life surrounding them, as unchanged as that in the remote Cornish fishing villages. The Lake District on the other hand, another of his subjects, was by then sophisticated and the home of elegant yachts, their white sails reflected in the still water as they passed with supreme grace across its surface.

Some of Frith's most memorable images are those which show the relationship, still surviving from the middle ages, of a river to a castle or cathedral. Lincoln Cathedral, towering above the town with the river below it, is striking and there are many other pictures, such as that of East Gate, King's Lynn, which are equally evocative.

The rivers and canals portrayed convey a sense of isolation, of slow movement and unhurried progress, even more acutely than the ports and fishing villages since these, however remote, are the centre of activity of some kind when ships come and go on the tide, for which there is no equivalent on land.

The paddle steamers that we have seen going around the coast had their inland equivalent and, although few of the original boats survive on the rivers they used to ply, one still survives on the Thames and another is being restored, and their successors still go up the most picturesque rivers just as they did before.

A tranquil summer's day on the Thames at Cliveden Reach. The steamer is the SS *Streatley*, and those on board must have been enjoying a perfect day as they passed along the river by the beech-clad slopes of the Cliveden estate on their way down to Windsor from Marlow. A trip on a river steamer such as this was considered a sublime way to spend an afternoon.

People took to the water more readily than they do now and rowing down from Oxford through this wonderful scenery was another popular choice. Baedeker's guide gave instructions and told you to get your boat 'from Salter Tims or Crissal of Oxford'. The boats were hired for a week which included the carriage of the boat back to Oxford.

The steamer trip shown here took three days on an unhurried journey to Kingston. Perhaps it was such an experience which inspired Frith to take one of his most evocative and beautiful photographs.

Frith's photograph of Lincoln can be read on a number of different levels. It is first of all a superb example of the kind of topographical photograph that the Victorians most admired. The cathedral towers above the town and is reflected finally in the waters of the River Witham.

The name of Lincoln is derived from an old British name meaning 'the hill fort by the pool', precisely the scene depicted here, with the cathedral on the site of the hill-fort, and the pool being the inland harbour which is in the forefront of the picture.

In the centre of the town is the last river bridge in England with medieval houses still on it. London Bridge, and countless other bridges in the past had on them houses, often built so close together that the ordinary traveller would not know that they were passing over a bridge. Lincoln's example is not on this scale but it is nonetheless a unique survival.

Of even greater antiquity is the Fossdyke Navigational Canal which is said to have been first excavated by the Romans. The inland port itself flourished in the middle ages with immense quantities of wool going over to Flanders for weaving. Here we see it in its later days. But the past has at least one echo in the sign on the right of the picture: 'H. Ward, Late Bell, Boatbbuilder. All kinds of boat for hire. Boats built to order'.

Paddle steamers were by no means confined to coastal trade. They plied inland waterways as well and fulfilled just as useful a function, either for day trips or for taking people from one place to another. This is the *Boston*, named after its setting with the tower of the famous Boston Stump, St. Botolph's, Boston, Lincolnshire, rising in the background. Judging by the people on the boat this is one of the routes that was used by local people going about their business, destined for one of the stops further up the River Witham.

On the other side of the Stump is the harbour at Boston which, as we shall see in the next chapter, still flourishes as a small port. The city of Boston in America is named after this town, and the links in its buildings and the people who were brought up here and made those early difficult trips to the New World are to be found on every hand. There is even a room in Fyddel House, one of the grandest houses in the town, known as the American Room, set aside for visitors from Boston, USA. The room was opened in 1938 by President Kennedy's father, then the American Ambassador to the Court of St. James.

The boat trip up the River Dart in Devon was one of the most popular in England, partly because of its great beauty, but also because it began at Dartmouth and all those visiting the cadets there invariably took this excursion. The journey took one and a quarter hours and cost one shilling and sixpence first class and one shilling and threepence second. Presumably the first-class passengers travelled in the front of the *Totnes Castle*, not a very large boat.

A good sign of the prosperity of the visitors can be seen in the very smart hotel coaches drawn up awaiting them. The two nearest belonged to the Castle Hotel and the Royal Seven Stars Hotel. Although this photograph was taken in 1896 the coaches' design is exactly that of the earliest London omnibuses of the middle years of the century. The brilliant lacquer work on the coaches is of such quality that reflections in it can be seen even from this distance, no doubt the proud work of a local coach-builder who, like the men who built the *Totnes Castle*, took justified pride in their work.

After pointing out that there is a train from Truro, Cornwall, to Falmouth, one well-known Victorian guidebook went on: 'A much pleasanter way of proceeding from Truro to Falmouth is by the little steamer which plies up and down the Fal every day'. The train was twice as fast, thirty minutes as opposed to an hour by boat, but the fare was less than a third for first class and only ninepence for those travelling second class. The crowd gathered here is obviously sure it has made the right choice and we see again the charming fashions just before the outbreak of the catastrophic First World War.

Quite by chance Frith has taken a photograph of two different Truros here. On the left is the 'little' steamer *Princess Victoria* with passengers prosperous and in the height of fashion; they have even had a new pavilion built for them the year before, in 1911, the date prominently displayed on its eaves. But on the right-hand side we see two commercial boats that have seen better days.

The view here could have been taken at any time in the previous thirty years, perhaps beyond. Some of the younger passengers already seem to find this old sailing boat of interest, and one young boy on the top deck is so enthusiastic about sail that he is holding up his model sailing boat for the photographer to admire and to make sure it got into the picture. He succeeded.

With their combination of elegance and speed, born of skilled handling and design, these yachts at Bowness, Lake Windermere, help explain why yachts and yacht racing are the one facet of maritime England that has remained an enthusiasm right up until today. Bowness is the head-quarters of the Royal Windermere Yacht Club and no doubt these yachts were their members' pride and joy. Windermere is the largest expanse of fresh water in Britain, which enabled designs of yachts to be refined and developed in races on its extensive waters. The spectators watching from their rowing boats tell us that we are watching a race in the 1890s, even if we had not been able to tell that from the boats' design. They also show that the enthusiasm for yachts was not confined to one social milieu: the cloth cap and bowler were a world away from the straw boaters on the other two boats. Once again, in one simple perfectly composed photograph, Frith gives us all the grace of the scene and a great deal more.

This scene unites in a charming way some very disparate elements. The elegant yachts in the distance and the girl in the foreground fishing in a full-length skirt contrast strongly for us today with the black coal smoke issuing from the stack of what must have been the most rudimentary form of steam ferry in existence. At the time the ferry caused no alarm or annoyance, and the girl fishes without noticing the disturbance in the water and the smoke. There were also many other steam launches on the lake, and the wisps of steam just visible by the yachts show two of them by the landing there. Nowadays there is a museum which preserves some of the most fascinating examples of these boats, supported by the Windermere Nautical Trust. Many of the larger passenger craft have been completely restored and are carrying people around the lake, with a break for afternoon tea, just as they always did. But the other side to this coin is that in places pollution of the lake and the damaging intrusion of too many tourists have become a real problem. The key to the transition from smoke pollution here, which was accepted, just as the smoke from trains in the countryside was accepted, to the unacceptable modern problem can be found in the ferry's load. Both are drawn by horse: the age of the motorcar was yet to come.

By contrast with the simple steam ferry at Lake Windermere, this at Fowey, Cornwall, the Bodinnick ferry, must be amongst the largest hand-operated ferries ever to be used. It looks as though it could carry about the same load as Windermere's. The bearded ferryman with his waistcoat must have had great strength and skill to manoeuvre his craft, with the help of his mate in the rear, resting on his oar for a moment. The sharp shadows show that they were working in hot sun at the height of the day. Despite all the advances of the twentieth century, simple ferries of this kind can still serve a purpose: there is one at Exeter today operated by a single man who pulls the ferry along a wire hawser strung across the river. Kept up by the Maritime Museum on the quay, it has existed continuously as a working ferry for centuries and is still used by ordinary people who want to cross the river.

21613. Dittisham, R. Dart.

Devon's River Dart at Dittisham just up river from Dartmouth, in 1889. Again Frith has taken a superbly evocative photograph, waiting for just the right moment on a day when the water was absolutely still and the smoke from the train on the far side of the valley was reflected perfectly in the river. The boatman here, in the simplest of sailing boats, looks like the ferryman of antiquity. The only prosaic element in the entire composition is the photographer's Gladstone bag sitting in the bottom of the boat.

Although the nationalized railways in England have now ceased using steam there are some companies that still run steam trains in the summer and the line along the banks of the Dart from Paignton to Kingsbridge opposite Dartmouth is one of them. The beauty of the valley and the impression left by such days as this have made some things sacred and worth keeping even if there is no great profit involved.

St Osyth on the River Colne in Essex, taken just before the outbreak of the First World War. There is not the slightest sign of the twentieth century in this charming view. Not a building, not a detail can be seen here that would not have looked exactly the same fifty or even a hundred years before, except the slowly changing line of the river's bank. The immense load of hay perhaps caught Frith's eye. It seems precariously balanced and almost too much for the boat, but loading and manoeuvring such vessels was a skill that boatmen had developed over the centuries and they knew instinctively what to load, and how to do it. St Osyth has the finest surviving group of monastic buildings in Essex and three Martello towers nearby.

Besides the Lake District the other great network of waterways that became a classic resort for those who wanted to spend time away from the busy world out on the water was the Norfolk Broads. It has now been discovered that these broads were formed in recent times as a result of extensive peat cutting in the middle ages. If this is so then it is an example, for once, of man's beneficial effect on his environment.

The Norfolk Broads were rich in wildlife and attracted that characteristic figure of the Victorian era, the amateur naturalist. The young man second from the right in this picture is holding a large butterfly net, and next to him is his specimen box. For the two men on the wherry *Widgeon*

he would have seemed an intrusion as much as the photographer on the opposite bank taking this view. Both the man in the hold and the man on deck have stopped work whilst the photograph is taken.

This mill at Horstead on the River Bure is typical of its kind, and, with the wherry servicing it, formed the cornerstone of the local economy, as they had done since the earliest times. The wherry evolved as the characteristic form of transport on the Broads, as easily recognizable as the Thames barge. The *Widgeon* is a basic commercial wherry. There were others converted to more domestic uses referred to as pleasure wherries.

The pleasure wherry *Rambler* at Horning Quay on the Norfolk Broads. The windows that have been let into the side of the boat for the converted accommodation can clearly be seen and, together with the incongruous garden bench perched on the bow, these indicate a boat used in leisurely travel around the Broads. The two caravans further along probably belong to those whose whole life was rambling, in those days called gipsies but now referred to as travellers. The owners have taken great trouble to make elaborate canvas coverings for them so it is likely that they were of the classic brilliantly painted type. By contrast, the hotel beyond is of the solid late Victorian kind and, with its garden on the river, canvas awnings and Lloyd Loom chairs, a picture of sophistication.

A perfect lazy day on an inland waterway, the old rowing boat sunk in the reeds in the foreground providing the perfect counterpoint to the windmill and wherry. The scene is at Coltishall, Norfolk, at the turn of the century.

Coltishall again, taken on the same day as the last photograph. The cob barns with thatched roofs are in the last stages of decay and yet are still being used, probably for storing the thatching reeds bundled up on the bank. Like the windmill, the buildings and crafts seen here had remained unchanged over the centuries.

A fishing competition at Horning, Norfolk. There are six boats visible, three in plain sight and three more beyond the wherry. No doubt the man in the wherry is the club secretary who will adjudicate the result and weigh the catches. The contrast between this leisurely way of spend- ing the afternoon and the lives of the fishermen around the coasts could not be greater. On the opposite bank a notice on the warehouse an- nounces that the owner deals in 'Corn, Coal and Pollard', staple elements in the local rural economy.

A fine view of Arundel Castle in West Sussex with the sweep of the River Arun before it. Frith has again chosen the ideal moment to take his photograph, waiting for the sailing barge to reach the centre of his picture where it balances the composition with the castle beyond.

The two men in the barge were the Victorian equivalent of the lorry driver and his mate. Their cargo appears to be stone and building materials, and transportation of heavy cargo of this kind was easier by river than by horse and cart and far more economical. The time taken was considerably longer than by road, and immensely longer than by railway, on the track seen running beside the river, but there was still a place for these men and the slower pace of their work.

The South Gate, King's Lynn, by an inlet of the River Mar. The gate was built in the 1520s and the scene here, with the Yarmouth ketch *Leader*, can have changed little over the centuries, apart from changes in the kind of craft. Today this inlet has been filled in and a small municipal garden constructed in its place. The gate is still much in use as one carriageway on the main London road. The car now dominates the scene entirely and the building on the right has gone, along with the ships it served. The gate itself is almost unchanged but only the building with the hipped roof on the left, a hostelry called the Honest Lawyer, can still be recognized today.

A working canal boat in another part of the country, the Springs Canal, Skipton, North Yorkshire. The boatman appears to be working his craft on his own and manoeuvring it along with the long poles all barges carried for keeping the craft off the banks, or away from the steep walls of a cutting, as here. Again, despite the date, 1910, heavy loads were still often carried by canal despite their gradual eclipse by the railways over the rest of the country. Skipton was a stopping place on the main Leeds to Liverpool Canal.

Surbiton near London in the 1890s with Messenger's boathouse on the opposite bank. In the foreground are two Thames spritsail barges, the *Glasgow* and the *James and Ann*, unloading cargoes of coal. The weight of the coal is obviously great: the *Glasgow* is so low in the water that she seems almost about to founder, but the men with her knew exactly what they were doing just as did those who oaded hay on to the barge at St Osyth (page 98). Anyone thinking of taking such loads by road when the river was close by would have seemed quite mad.

Photographs of working men carrying out ordinary work day tasks at this period are not common. When Frith took this picture he cannot have imagined that it would one day have such fascination, and such genuine historical interest.

The Manchester Ship Canal, the greatest canal of all, thirty-six miles long and only opened in 1894 to link Manchester with the sea and make her an inland port of major importance. The Runcorn Bridge crosses the canal here, towards the end of its journey. The construction of the canal was one of the great triumphs of Victorian initiative and skill. The view here has echoes of the great river projects normally undertaken abroad such as the Victoria Bridge in Montreal. The canal has recently been set on a completely new commercial footing and will reach its centenary with as good hopes for its future as memories of its great past.

The Pomana Dock at Manchester at the turn of the century showing the ocean-going merchant schooner *Trevellas* on the right of the picture. The authority on merchant schooners, Basil Greenhill, said of her: 'To this day, seamen of the west coast speak of her speed and handiness ... She remained a three-masted schooner until 1929 when she was fitted with power'. She had a sad ending typical of so many ships over the ages, leaving Port Talbot in November 1930 to be lost at sea without any further word of her. Ocean-going ships, of which the steam vessels opposite were more typical, came to Manchester along the famed Manchester Ship Canal which ensured that Manchester remained one of the foremost industrial centres of the country in the face of growing rivalry, and the position of Liverpool as a major port.

Chapter Eight
COASTAL TRADE

England's coastline affords myriad points of shelter and from the earliest days any river mouth, bay or natural harbour has been explored and its full possibilities established by local people over generations. All these places, from London which was created by the Thames, to such ports as Bristol, reached through the narrow Clifton Gorge, or Liverpool on the Mersey, down to the smallest fishing village in Cornwall, responded to the need for transport for the inland community and for stopping-off places for people travelling abroad or returning to England.

The nineteenth century brought about a major change in the delicate balance between rival ports, and that was because of the railway. Any port which had a railway going to it would immediately dominate a rival which had no railway or an inferior service. The example of Southampton and Weymouth is well known. Long time rivals for services to France and the Channel Islands, Southampton gained an inestimable advantage with the arrival of the railway and Weymouth never managed to catch up. Similar examples can be found all over the country. Much of the coastal trade in such commodities as coal and feedstuffs was conducted by the merchant schooners already mentioned; flourishing ports took on the larger metal ships – the familiar coasters. However, as long as the sailing ships continued to exist and there were things for them to transport, then they too continued to do so, however small the scale, and however much the large ports grew.

The contrast between the paddle steamers with their cargoes of passengers only, all of whom could be picked up at an elegant pier's end, and the commercial vessels was great. Cargo required handling; it required transport to take it away from the docks as soon as possible and it required a skilled dockside force to deal with different kinds of cargoes.

The distinction between ports that were large but not of the largest scale, and the unquestionably great ports is sometimes not simple, especially at the time Frith worked, when new ports were being constructed. The same would be true today, with someone even twenty years ago being shocked at the disappearance of London and the appearance of such ports as Felixstowe. Here we have simply taken Frith's photographs as a guide.

Frith's photographers visited every port in the country of whatever size and we show a range of these, chosen either for their intrinsic interest as photographs or because of the importance of the ports depicted.

The shock of the new in Bideford, North Devon, in 1907 – a motorcar, with a striking circular chrome surround on its radiator. The two tracks just visible on the road surface in the background are for a light railway running into the town.

Bideford was once a great port, the busiest in North Devon with a great trade to North America; in the churchyard is the grave of an American Indian who was brought back from America by Sir Richard Grenville. Today there is little business of any great scale transacted.

The town is best known for its position on the River Torridge, and the fourteenth century bridge of twenty-four arches, spanning the estuary. Its literary claim to fame is that the author Charles Kingsley wrote a great part of his book *Westward Ho!* here in 1854.

Baedeker's guidebook majestically remarked 'The town itself contains little to arrest the tourist'. This may have had the incidentally beneficial effect of keeping it off the beaten track, as a tranquil haven, which is how it appears here, with just one motorcar as a warning of things to come.

Frith showed a typical Victorian's view of the world and, when photographing Fowey in Cornwall, did not stop at the picturesque views, the regatta and the old-world ferry. Here he shows the shipping of china clay, the source of Fowey's wealth as a port. The rows of piers are not for social promenading by holidaymakers or tourists but for railway trucks bringing the raw material to the end of the piers where steam cranes lowered the clay into lighters or directly to the large commercial sailing ships, still in use as we see here, or metal steamers. The picturesque countryside around is still unspoiled by this activity and would remain so as long as ships were the main method of transport rather than lorries.

We have seen earlier the fisherfolk of West Looe, Cornwall. Here is a bird's-eye view of the other side of the river, East Looe, which was far more commercial and represented the kind of dock at which the coastal-trading merchant schooners called. A schooner is seen coming into the port here.

In front of the prosperous new warehouses are railway tracks and a number of trucks with what looks like coal in them. The presence of a railway line was vital to continuing activity in a commercial port and when this photograph was taken in 1889 small ports without a rail connection were losing out to ports such as this that had one. In the end there was a limit to the expansion of this port in which the decline in merchant schooner traffic must have played an important part.

There was fishing in East Looe as well of course and just in front of the new warehouses nets can be seen spread out over the quay and in front of them, by the slipway, a group of fish-wives with their white aprons can clearly be made out.

This is Calstock, Cornwall, again, just downriver from the shipyard and the building of the new viaduct (see picture page 82). The signs of a busy trade appear on the quay, stone on the left, timbers in the centre and coal carefully banked up on the right. A railway line with a single truck can be seen on the far right of the picture.

Today all this has gone. The 'square' which is here covered with materials is now tidy and grass verged and the only people who arrive are visitors who are going to see the exquisite Cotehele House just a little way up the river on the left or to take part in canoeing or amateur sailing. There is still a river boat in the season, but ships like the merchant schooner on the left are no more.

The training ship *Foudroyant* (left) at Falmouth, Cornwall, in 1918. The third ship to bear this name, she was originally the *Trincomalee*, a fifth-rate warship built at Bombay in 1817. Her predecessor had been one of Nelson's flagships, eventually bought by a Mr. Wheatley Cobb from her subsequent German owners and turned into a training ship. When she was destroyed by accident in a fire in 1897 her owner acquired the *Trincomalee* and converted her in turn into a training ship with the new name *Foudroyant*. Today, although currently being refitted in Sunderland, she is normally to be found at Portsmouth where she still acts as a training ship. Beyond her in this typically calm scene of Frith's is the port of Falmouth which also survives, still flourishing, and moving forward to even greater prominence.

Here is evidence in 1930 of Falmouth's prosperity when other ports were in difficulty. It is not possible to identify the steam ships in the harbour, but the sailing ship in the foreground could be recognized on sight by any who have visited her at her dry dock on the Thames at Greenwich. It is not exactly chance that Frith's man has got the *Cutty Sark* in his lens. She had first appeared in Falmouth eight years before, in 1922, when she was forced to take shelter there on her way from London to Lisbon after a refit; her owners at that time were Portuguese. Whilst in the harbour she was noticed by Captain Wilfred Downer. He acted in much the same spirit as Mr. Wheatley Cobb (see previous picture), bought her and set about repairing her where necessary and restoring her to her original rig. After Captain Downer's death she spent some time as a training ship moored at Greenhithe before eventually going to Greenwich under a scheme sponsored by the local council. She was opened to the public in 1957 and countless thousands have looked over her since then. We see her here after the last genuinely commercial voyage she took.

Falmouth's landing stage and port show every sign of being as busy at the beginning of the century when this photograph was taken as it is now at the end of it. The merchant schooner, whose masts can be seen here, is a thing of the past but for the rest there are modern echoes. Scrap metal, although it always seems to remind us of the present and the modern industrial world, has existed as long as the iron industry and its products have existed and the scrap piled on the ground here is no doubt shortly going by railway trucks, rather than lorry, to the smelting furnaces of the 'black country' to start its life again.

Although the ship whose funnel can just be seen in the background dwarfed the merchant schooner in front of it at the quay, it would itself be overshadowed entirely by the size of the ships that call at Falmouth today. Even an 'industrial' scene such as this has its element of nostalgia.

Boston, Lincolnshire, is another town that has survived as a commercial port to the present day. There has been surprisingly little change since the scene pictured here, in the 1890s. The capstan on which the men in the foreground are leaning has gone but the dock itself and the striking bank of warehouses at the end of the dock are all exactly the same. The biggest change has been on the right. Although the dock remains the same size it has been transformed by the introduction of machinery for handling containers which runs down its length. It is a reminder of the changing world of land transport that where the railway trucks seen here used to take the bulk cargo there are now lorries, being laden with entire containers at once and driven off along already congested roads.

As in the fishing communities (see Chapter 3) a striking difference can be seen in the clothing, which is of much higher quality than would be worn today, although sociologists would no doubt assign this to cultural changes rather than the general drop in the standard of living.

Weymouth harbour, Dorset, at the turn of the century. The transport historian P J Perry has commented shrewdly on the reason for Weymouth's relative decline at this time in favour of its old rival Southampton: 'The railways were a major determinant of the fortunes of many British ports, large and small, especially during the nineteenth century … When the railway reached Southampton in 1840 Weymouth soon lost a great deal of traffic, notably the Channel Island mails … throughout this period it had officially been accepted that Southampton had gained no more than a temporary advantage – in fact its effects were to last for about fifty years.' Today Southampton is once again a main departure point for the Channel Islands, but at this time there was clearly little going on. The only ship identifiable here is that on the right, the brigantine *Estafette*. The painted sign just above her is of considerable interest for it announces 'Best Norwegian Ice'. This is not a trade term but genuine ice from Norway which was a major import for much of the last century and some way into this. The National Maritime Museum has recently published a monograph on this forgotten trade. This detail on one of Frith's photographs, captured by chance, shows the value of his images from a genuinely historical standpoint providing direct evidence where none would otherwise exist.

The Avon Gorge at Clifton, with Leigh Woods on the left, a photograph by Frith probably taken from the famous Clifton Suspension Bridge designed by Brunel but not completed until four years after his death. When this picture was taken the gorge was still being used by the many ships going to and from the port of Bristol. The ships seen here are all dredgers whose work was essential to keep the passage open.

The gorge has seen the beginning of many historic voyages: John and Sebastian Cabot set sail from Bristol for the New World in 1497. The rib of a whale which they brought back is preserved in the church of St Mary Redcliffe, the grandest parish church in England, very near the tomb and armour of Admiral Penn, father of William Penn (the founder of Pennsylvania).

In modern times the gorge saw the passage of such famous ships as Brunel's SS *Great Britain*, launched in Bristol and recently returned there to its original dry dock where it is being completely restored.

The striking view has attracted many painters over the years, notably Francis Danby who painted it from almost exactly this spot.

Ramsgate harbour, Kent, showing the Victorian equivalent of a maritime traffic jam. The serpentine sweep of the white stone balustrading on brick pillars and arches is typical of the unsung elegancies of Victorian civic architecture. The mobile steam crane at work on the left of the picture shows that, although all the vessels are sailing ships, industry has made some inroads on the scene. Just visible at the quayside is one of the merchant schooners that played a vital role in coastal trade through Frith's lifetime.

Although somewhat grander than nearby Margate, Ramsgate was still a favourite haunt for Londoners on excursion rail tickets. George Eliot called it 'a strip of London out for an airing', but it also had fine hotels such as the Granville, designed by A W Pugin and boasting that ultimate Victorian luxury – a Turkish bath.

Folkestone, Kent, and the prominently sited London and Paris Hotel announces the main business of the port. An interesting feature of the building is an original penthouse on its roof. The harbours contain a general mixture of shipping typical of 1895, with a paddle steamer, various other steamers and two schooners, one under repair.

Folkestone is one of those few places whose entry in the guidebooks has remained unchanged through a century or more. Baedeker in 1887 referred to it as a channel ferry port with a fishing port running alongside it, and a modern guide remarks, 'the harbour is still a working harbour for cross-channel steamers and fishing boats'. The detail changes, such as the railway coaches at the end of the pier, but the spirit of the place seems to have remained much the same.

The *Ingoldsby Legends* have a passing reference to Folkestone as a 'collection of houses which its malingers call a fishing town and its well-wishers a watering place'. This photograph of the fishing port in 1912 shows evidence for both points of view, for we see both a working fishing town and elegant Edwardian sophistication.

The proprietor of the chandlery, posing languidly in the doorway of the seventeenth-century timber building in his bow-tie and three-piece suit, would have seemed out of place in a city bank even then; today his clothes would pass muster at a diplomatic reception. Even the driver of the trap waiting for his fare to finish her conversation, perhaps with Mr Pierce himself, whose name appears on the fish-boxes and the faded sign, has a smart cap and a briar pipe instead of a clay one.

A fine view of Dover in Kent from the Belle Vue Tea Gardens at the turn of the century. The ferry port here is on an immense scale already, with construction still continuing. One interesting fact that distinguished this time from ours is that it was still the practice to use convict labour for public works of this kind, and convicts were actually used in the work seen proceeding on the horizon. Steamers left here for Calais three times a day and for Ostend twice a day.

As the central port for passage to the Continent before the coming of the aeroplane, there can hardly have been a writer or politician of note who had not passed through. Henry James began writing *The Bostonians* here; the first serving American president to come to England, Woodrow Wilson, landed here; and of the more unusual crossings at this point Captain Webb set out from Dover twenty-five years before on the first cross-channel swim.

❧ Chapter Nine ❧
HISTORIC SHIPS AND GREAT PORTS

Today the commercial cargoes coming into Britain and leaving for export are greater both in worth and volume than they have ever been. The monthly balance of trade exceeds by many times an entire year's figures from Frith's time. And yet there is a great difference in public consciousness of these ports and the part they play in the country's life.

The reasons for this are not difficult to find. They are illustrated most graphically by the case of Liverpool. Here the great transatlantic liners used to bring people from the New World to the Old, and see hopeful immigrants set out for the New in search of opportunities that their homeland could not give them.

Nowadays all transatlantic journeys except for the luxury cruises that take only a handful of people are made by jet planes. Their runways are inland and what you are passing over in flight is of little consequence. The countries of the pacific rim are separated by immense areas of water, yet when flying over Australia to Singapore, for example, if there is any sort of cloud cover there is no way of telling whether you are flying over Australian desert or ocean. Even if the atmosphere is clear you are usually too high to see anything of importance.

This modern world is as different as can be from the world that Frith belonged to. Passengers at Liverpool would be aware of every detail of their journey and all but the most completely disinterested would learn countless facts about the sea and the maritime life going on around them. It is this element more than any other that needs to be understood when looking at these photographs and following their significance. The only modern substitute is the car ferry, and that is no substitute at all. Only in places such as Piraeus in Greece is the density of ship traffic and the frequency of travel to the islands enough to give some idea of what every busy British port must have been like.

It is difficult to tell what effect this change in the nation's psyche, if it can be called that, has had. The commercial shipping continues but the general public, the travelling public that would have been part of it, has no experience of it. By contrast, for every family before the war, and going back into the earliest days of British history, sea travel formed part of its life. In the middle ages there were travelling merchants or ecclesiastics, or doctors who were trained abroad; in later centuries there were the 'box-wallahs' or Civil Service men going to India; then there were the sailors themselves or the forces going to anywhere in what is now called the Commonwealth.

There has been a rapid falling-off of the essentially maritime character of the British people that a marginal increase in the purchase of boats in marinas will not halt. It may be no coincidence that at the same time there appears to be increased identification with Europe, and the Continent as a whole. A brief plane flight takes us from one land-mass to another effortlessly and the experience creates the illusion of one vast continent of which we are a part. The old habits of mind of an island race are slowly whittled away.

Frith's photographs of the larger ports – only a small selection is possible here of course, chosen as before for their overall quality and interest – show the world before this process had begun. The commercial docks and international ports were as much part of people's lives then as any other aspect of life in England, and everyone had in common a closeness to and dependence on the sea.

When Frith reached Portsmouth in Hampshire his rigid adherence to topographical principles finally had to give way to Britain's maritime heritage and he found himself photographing ships not places.

Michael Shea has remarked: 'Portsmouth was, and is, Britain's premier naval base', and this was undoubtedly the case when this photograph was taken (c1890). Foremost was HMS *Victory*, Nelson's flagship at Trafalgar. The *Oxford Companion to Ships and the Sea*, edited by Peter Kemp, gives a full account of the ship and the four previous ships to bear her name. At this stage, although recognized as an historic

ship, no attempts were being made to bring her back on historical principles to her condition in the days of Trafalgar. It was sufficient that she was still afloat, and repairs were limited to those that would keep her so, and that is how she is seen here. Later, in 1922, she was given an extensive refit and moved to Portsmouth dry dock where she now is.

There is a further refit going on at the present time, the most extensive since that in 1922, but the public may still visit her, which they do in great numbers.

Another view of the harbour, taken on the same day as the picture of HMS *Victory* (see previous picture). Here we see HMS *Duke of Wellington*. Along side her are two hulks, dark forbidding objects that were conceived of originally as convict ships. There were some on the Thames opposite what is now the Tate Gallery, then Millbank prison, which kept prisoners prior to their deportation. These here were also used for quarantine patients, and as stores. The National Maritime Museum identifies the hulk on the left as *Belvidere* and that on the right as probably *Tyrian*.

An evocative photograph of Portsmouth taken in about 1890 and one of the last occasions when a view of this kind could have been taken with so many of the old ships on a large expanse of water looking much as they must have done at the time of Trafalgar. The nearest is HMS *St Vincent*, then a training ship.

HMS *St Vincent* again but her surroundings in sharp contrast to those in the last paragraph. Although taken only some twelve years later, in 1902, the scene seems an age away. This is partly the setting, with the ferries plying in front of the *St Vincent*, and a steam ship beyond, but also the commercial atmosphere, with mass advertising taking a strong hold. The booking kiosk for the New Steam Launch Company unwittingly sets the tone for the coming century with its dreadnoughts and submarines and, eventually nuclear submarines. The *St Vincent* is already here a symbol of a vanished age.

If Portsmouth was always the premier naval port, then Plymouth in Devon ran it a close second for many years. In Elizabethan times it was undoubtedly the most important, and in America is always the first Old-World port to spring to mind for it was from here that the Pilgrim Fathers sailed in 1620. Sir Francis Drake sailed from Plymouth on 13 December 1577 on his voyage around the world, and it was on the Hoe, seen here, that the fabled incident of his refusing to be disturbed from his game of bowls by news of the Spanish Armada took place. *The Oxford* *Companion to Ships and the Sea* shrewdly points out that the remarks attributed to Drake are first recorded in 1736 and are perhaps therefore to be doubted. Plymouth men however would say that oral history was invented in Devon and Drake's action is as true as anything is likely to be.

The lighthouse seen here is the original stone one, moved here at the end of the last century. The scene is not greatly changed today, although the pier, from which this view was taken, in 1902, has now gone.

Plymouth adjoins the great naval dockyard of Devonport. For many years these three ships, known as *The Establishment* were anchored at Devonport and served as training ships. The actual ships varied, as did their order, and a detailed study of them can be seen at the National Maritime Museum.

The atmosphere is not noticeably different from that in the earlier photographs of Portsmouth, but this view was taken in 1913. A few years later German battle cruisers would be steaming down the east coast of Britain shelling towns as they went, and the British Fleet would have engaged German ships in the first Falklands engagement. The fact that so many of the sailors had trained in old sailing ships did not detract from their performance one whit, and sailing training ships, tall ships, exist today all over the world following on the old traditions in an age of nuclear power just as they were learnt here.

Besides its history and its naval dockyards, Plymouth was, and is, a flourishing commercial and fishing port. This 1893 view of Sutton Pool in the docks, with the Barbican behind, shows a typical range of every kind of ship. By the Barbican is the SS *Newcastle*; on the left is the ketch *Bonetta*; behind her is the schooner *Niels*; and part of the fishing fleet is in the centre of the pool. Plymouth's Barbican survives today just as it was here, and not much changed from the time when Drake knew it, but the rest of the town is almost entirely new, rebuilt after its almost total destruction in air-raids in the Second World War.

A similarly flourishing scene but of an entirely different kind from the last photograph, on the other side of the country at Hull in Humberside. Baedeker remarked of Hull in another of his disdainful asides: 'Though a place of considerable antiquity it possesses few old buildings and offers little to detain the tourist'. At the time that was written Hull had a deep-sea fishing fleet of five hundred boats and was *the* trading port between England and northern Europe. Baedeker was in fact warning his readers that Hull was part of the 'real' world, from which most of them were trying to escape. The view here shows a wide range of shipping that just happened to come into Frith's viewfinder, besides the very elaborate two-level Victorian Pier. The old sailing ship at the top left of the picture is the training ship *Southampton*; the modern warship is HMS *Dido*; and behind the pier, out of sight, is a steamer which the crowds are waiting to board. The sailing vessel is a Humber sloop.

Alexandra Dock, Hull. It was scenes such as this that epitomized Hull and which would have gladdened the heart of any Victorian or Edwardian industrialist who knew how the country's wealth was really made. However romantic the sight of a fishing fleet under sail, it brought only fish home. This sight represented the culmination of engineering skill and commercial enterprise which gave Britain and her merchant navy world leadership. It is open to debate as to how much the attitudes of the 'tourist' who avoid such places, attitudes slowly seeping through from the upper strata of society downwards, actively contributed to Britain's loss of this position not so long after this was taken.

Hull, 1930. Anyone trying to find this exact view today will have some difficulty. The only building actually remaining as it was here is the three-domed harbour office. The Wilberforce column, commemorating William Wilberforce the anti-slavery campaigner who was born in Hull, has been moved to a spot by the University. The docks have been filled in or converted and many of the buildings have been rebuilt since the war.

One welcome change, with the passing of steam and coal, has been that the dark pall of soot in which all the buildings here were covered year in year out has been removed. The first stage in the new civic awareness which has given a new face to many old cities is the removal of this layer of soot and grime. Note too the absence of the modern advertising industry, only the one word OXO amusingly intruding into a scene free from today's multi-coloured hoardings.

Barry Docks, South Glamorgan, are a late example of that kind of explosive industrial development which characterized the earlier years of Victoria's reign, and the cities of the New World. In 1880 Barry was a village with precisely eighty-five inhabitants. In 1887 a guidebook, while talking of the five miles of quays in Cardiff, mentioned in passing that 'additional' docks were being built at Barry. The first dock opened in 1889 and a second dock soon followed. By the time this was taken, in about 1899, they were already booming and Barry was the most important coal port in the country, featuring full mechanization; a moveable coal tip can be seen on the right.

King's Dock, Swansea, West Glamorgan, in the 1920s, thriving before the crash of 1929 and subsequent slump. The great steel mills of Margam and Port Talbot nearby provided the main industrial focus for this part of Wales and during the war drew the German airforce in raids which wreaked great havoc.

There are today over six miles of quays at Swansea and the ships that dock there are from a different era to the steamers seen here. The SS *Kepwick Hall*, registered at West Hartlepool, in the centre of the picture, is a reminder of the days when the British merchant fleet dominated shipping and 'flags of convenience' were hardly known.

The smoke billowing from the tug would nowadays give the environmentally conscious a reminder of the days when coal powered ships rather than diesel, but smoke and soot were as much a part of working life here as the mining of coal was to the Welsh economy.

The docks at Middlesbrough, Cleveland, c1913, the view dominated by the transporter bridge, perhaps the most startling way of taking passengers across a river.

Middlesbrough began life at the start of the nineteenth century with a population of fewer than a hundred people. The Stockton and Darlington Railway and the discovery of iron in the Cleveland Hills transformed it into the capital of the Cleveland iron district.

Although some abhorred this kind of transformation and talked of 'dark Satanic mills' (although Blake was actually describing churches), there were plenty of other Victorians who took immense pride in the skills and enterprise exhibited by the great ironmasters and workmen. They would see in the slender lines of this bridge as much elegance as others would find in the sweeping lines of the vault of a cathedral. As remarked when talking of Hull (see page 133), the picturesque fishing villages which many found so nostalgic were, for other Victorians, places they were only too glad to have escaped from. Rather thriving industry than picturesque poverty any time even if the old adage 'where there's muck there's brass' was often only true when read the other way about.

The landing stages at Liverpool from the Mersey, c1895. Travelling to America at this time was simply a matter of arriving at Liverpool, finding a ship, of which there were many, paying five pounds, and going. Passports and other controls did not exist and would have seemed a nightmare beyond even the imaginings of George Orwell in *Nineteen Eighty Four*. It is refreshing to look at a photograph such as this and realize that life in all its most complex forms could go on entirely without such costly bureaucratic burdens, an invention of the twentieth century.

The steamship on the left here is the SS *Lucania*, and just behind her the paddle steamer *Ben My Chree*. The landing stage was over two thousand feet long and connected to the shore by eight bridges, some of which can be made out here. The north end of this pier was known as Prince's Pier, and sea-going steamers usually left from there. The south end, George's Pier, dealt with the river ferry boats, the ferry across the Mersey, for example, later to be made famous in a Liverpool popular song.

George's Landing Stage, Liverpool, with the entrance to the Birkenhead Ferry on the extreme left, in about 1895. There are signs here that the much-talked-of Edwardian elegance was simply a development of late-Victorian success, for every clerk has his bowler set at a rakish angle, and there are even top hats and velvet collars to be seen amongst the crowd.

The flourishing business community is the complement of the feverish activity in the city's docks and factories, and it is interesting to notice that, unlike today, there are almost no ladies to be seen.

The Customs House, Liverpool, in 1888, with a corner of Canning Dock in front of it. This was the oldest dock in existence in Liverpool, opened in 1717. The very first dock was on the site occupied by the Customs House and other Revenue departments.

Again, to modern eyes, the quay seems almost deserted, but this is simply the absence of motorized-transport and the general flux of sight-seers and lookers-on. In fact, no fewer than twelve horses can be counted here, and it would have been they that pulled the heavy loads such as the boiler and other metalwork to the quay.

In the foreground the schooner *Louisa* has a man in her rigging, presumably a common enough sight at the time, but one rarely seen in Frith's negatives.

Another vital facet of a great port, the dry docks. This is Liverpool's Langton Graving Dock, one of a number of graving docks in the port with the SS *Cherbourg*. Just visible in the background is the Liverpool Overhead Railway which opened in 1893, two years before this view was taken.

City of Chicago, 5,202 tons, built in 1883 by C Connell and Co of Glasgow for the Inman Line. Shortly afterwards the Inman Line passed into the ownership of the International Navigation Company and together they became known as the 'I and I', the Inman and International Steam Ship Company.

The company had six ships competing on the prestigious transatlantic route at the time this photograph was taken. Cunard held the record for the fastest crossing, with the White Star and I and I lines making determined challenges.

Although one of the best ships afloat when launched, the *City of Chicago* was soon surpassed. When she was wrecked in 1892 she had been totally overshadowed by her sister ship, the *City of New York*.

The *City of New York*, built in 1888 by James and George Thomson of Glasgow for the Inman and International Steam Ship Company. She was designed by Sir John Biles as an express twin-screw liner and was the first such boat to be completed. She has been described as 'the largest, fastest, most luxurious and most beautiful liner in the world'.

Shortly after this photograph was taken she and the White Star liner *Teutonic* competed in one of the most famous transatlantic races. On 4 September 1890 she left England at 2.45pm, the *Teutonic* leaving minutes later at 2.58. When they arrived in New York on the 10th the *Teutonic* had gained five minutes on the *City of New York*! On the voyage back

the *Teutonic* increased her margin to twelve minutes. Although she lost on this occasion, the *City of New York* did achieve a record in 1892 making the first eastward crossing in less than six days – in 5 days, 19 hours and 57 minutes. From then on she was surpassed, although lasting well into the next century, fighting in the Spanish-American War as the *Harvard*, and during the First World War as the *Plattsburg*, armed with three 6in and two 3in guns, and finally bringing Italian immigrants to America until she was scrapped in 1932.

She is seen here at the very height of her fame.